Excel Works

Making the most of Microsoft® Excel

GW01185370

FOLENS

Patricia Harrison   **Papia Sarkar**

Dear Reader,

ICT is changing everyone's lives. At work, in the home, and in school, what we do and how we do it has been transformed by the use of computers. The most widely used spreadsheet package around the world is Microsoft® **Excel**. In writing this book, we have taken the 50 most important functions of **Excel**, which will be of help to you in your work in school.

Each left-hand page takes you step-by-step through a single function. The screenshots help you to recognise on your screen what you are seeing on the page. These pages are called **skill** pages and can be used to learn the skill and to refer back to, whatever you are doing, to remind yourself of how to carry out a function.

Skills are only useful if you can use them to improve your work. Each right-hand page therefore provides an opportunity to apply your skill in a practical context. These are called **Application** pages. Once you have learned and applied a skill, you should look for opportunities in your school work to apply this skill regularly. In this way it will become second nature to you. Your work will improve not just in Maths and Science but across the whole curriculum.

Enjoy the book and be confident that if you learn from it, your attainment will increase.

Best wishes

Patricia   Papia

Contents

Opening a New Workbook and Entering Text

Opening a new workbook

1 Click **File**.

2 Click **New**.

3 Click the **General** tab.

File
New...	Ctrl+N
Open...	Ctrl+O
Save As...	
Page Setup...	
Print...	Ctrl+P
1 Mel Radcliff - Class List	
2 Jake Adam - Class List	
3 Ivor Longarm - Class List	
4 Ibraheem Batan - Class List	

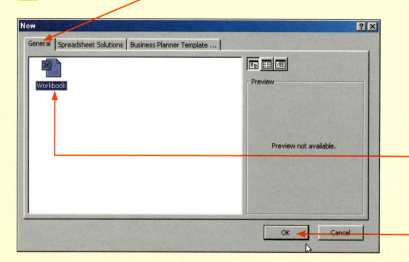

4 Click **Workbook**.

5 Click **OK**.

A **New** workbook will open.

Entering text

6 Type your text.

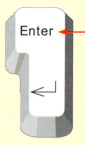

7 Press **Enter** to move down to the next **Cell**.

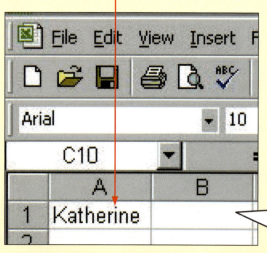

*If you want to move to the **Cell** on the right, use the **Arrow** keys or point and click on the **Cell** in which you want to enter text.*

1b

APPLICATION

SKILL: Opening a New Workbook and Entering Text

1 Open a **New** workbook. (See 1a)

2 Type your full name.

3 Press **Enter**.

4 Type your class name or number.

5 Press **Enter** twice. This will leave a blank row.

6 Type the forename of a member of your class.

7 Press **Enter**.

8 Type the forenames of another 10 members of your class. Remember to press **Enter** after each entry.

9 **Save** your work.

10 **Print** your work.

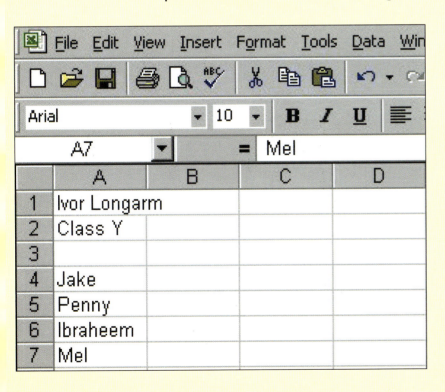

> **Remember**
> *You can use the icons at the top of your screen to open a **New** workbook and **Save**.*

New

Save

ExcelWorks

2a Opening an Existing Workbook and Editing Entries

SKILL

Opening an existing workbook

1 Click **File**.

2 Click **Open**.

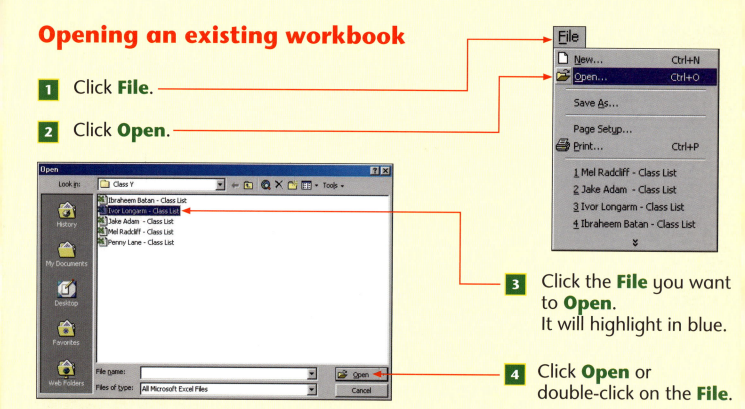

3 Click the **File** you want to **Open**.
It will highlight in blue.

4 Click **Open** or double-click on the **File**.

Editing entries

5 Click the **Cell** that you want to change.

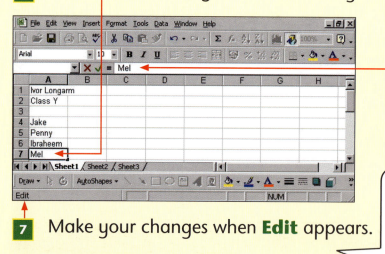

6 Move and click the cursor I on the **Formula Bar** where you want to change your entry.

7 Make your changes when **Edit** appears.

8 Press **Enter**.

You can also:
a. Double-click on the **Cell** that you want to change.
b. In the **Cell**, move the cursor to where you want to make your change.

Excel Works

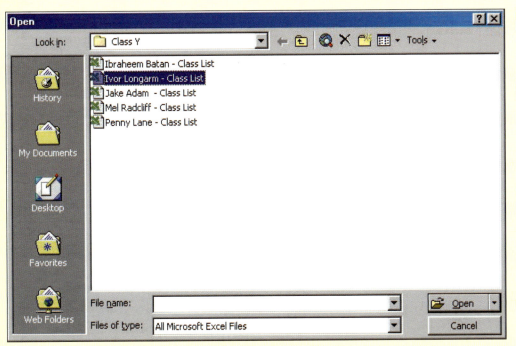

1 **Open** your 'Class List' File. (See 2a)

2 **Edit** the first five names on your list by adding the surnames.

3 **Close** the File.

4 **Edit** your list by adding surnames to the rest of the forenames. This time, use the icon at the top of the screen to **Open** the File.

Open

5 **Save** your work.

6 **Print** your work.

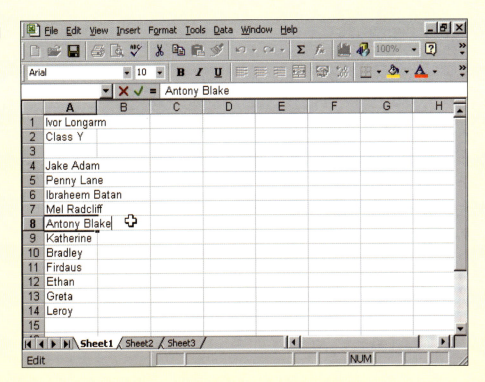

1 Open a **New** workbook. (See 1a)

2 Click **Format**.

3 Click **Cells**.

4 Click the **Font** tab.

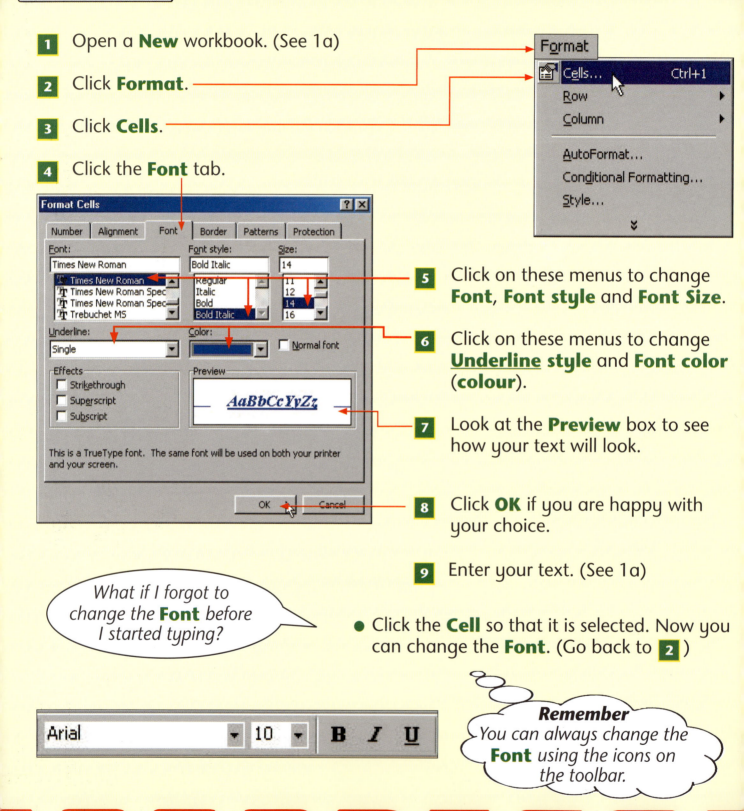

5 Click on these menus to change **Font**, **Font style** and **Font Size**.

6 Click on these menus to change **Underline** style and **Font color** (**colour**).

7 Look at the **Preview** box to see how your text will look.

8 Click **OK** if you are happy with your choice.

9 Enter your text. (See 1a)

*What if I forgot to change the **Font** before I started typing?*

● Click the **Cell** so that it is selected. Now you can change the **Font**. (Go back to **2**)

Remember
You can always change the ***Font*** *using the icons on the toolbar.*

Change your Class List

SKILL: Changing Font, Font Size, Font Style and Font Colour

3b

APPLICATION

1 **Open** your 'Class List' File. (See 2a)

2 In a different **Column**, add the name of the street where each of the people in your class lives.

3 Change the **Font**, **Font style** and **Font colour** of the names. (See 3a)

4 Change the **Font**, **Font style** and **Font colour** of the street names.

Bradley Hand ITC	▼	12	▼	**B**	*I*	U̲						%						A		

A1	▼	=	Ivor Longarm

	A	B	C	D	E	F	G	H
1	*Ivor Longarm*							
2	Class Y							
3								
4	*Jake Adam*		Deepdale Road					
5	*Penny Lane*		Whitehart Lane					
6	*Ibraheem Batan*		Lane Ends					
7	*Mel Radcliff*		Liverpool Road					
8	*Antony Blake*		Elland Road					
9	*Katherine Green*		Mayfair Street					
10	*Bradley Metcalf*		Cross Roads					
11	*Firdaus Patel*		Fisher Lane					
12	*Ethan Miles*		St Georges Way					
13	*Greta Overmann*		Kings Street					
14	*Leroy Wayne*		Riverside					
15	*Jade Bamber*		Victoria Lane					
16	*Harrison Patrick*		Capital Road					
17								
18								

5 **Save** your work.

6 **Print** your work.

Excel*Works*

4a SKILL

Entering Numbers in Cells

1 Open a **New** workbook. (See 1a)

2 Click the **Cell** where you want your number to be placed.

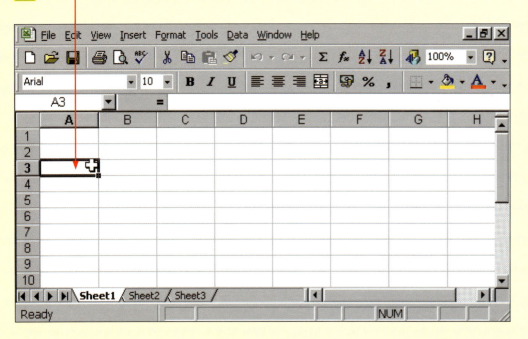

3 Type your number.

4 Press **Enter** to move your cursor to the **Cell** below.

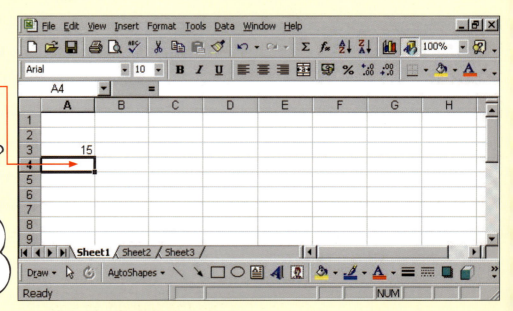

> **Remember**
> If you want to enter a number in the **Cell** to the right, point and click on it or use the **Arrow** keys.

Shoe Sizes

SKILL: Entering Numbers in Cells

4b

APPLICATION

1 **Open** the 'Class List' File. (See 2a)

2 In the **Column** in which the street names were entered, add the house numbers. (See 4a)

3 In a new **Column**, add the shoe size of each pupil on your list.

4 Choose a different **Font colour** for each shoe size. (See 3a)

	A	B	C	D	E	F	G
1	Ivor Longarm					6	
2	Class Y						
3							
4	Jake Adam		15 Deepdale Road			6	
5	Penny Lane		100 Whitehart Lane			2	
6	Ibraheem Batan		23 Lane Ends			4	
7	Mel Radcliff		576 Liverpool Road			3	
8	Antony Blake		2 Elland Road			5	
9	Katherine Green		99 Mayfair Street			3	
10	Bradley Metcalf		89 Cross Roads			3	
11	Firdaus Patel		56 Fisher Lane			4	
12	Ethan Miles		44 St Georges Way			5	
13	Greta Overmann		27 Kings Street			2	
14	Leroy Wayne		73 Riverside			7	
15	Jade Bamber		29 Victoria Lane			2	
16	Harrison Patrick		8 Capital Road			4	
17							

5 **Save** your work.

6 **Print** your work.

> **Remember**
> *You can also use the numbers on the keypad on your keyboard.*

Selecting Ranges

1 Enter this data or use your own.

2 Click and hold the mouse in the first **Cell** in the **Range**.

3 Drag across all the **Cells** you want in your **Range**.

> *A group of **Cells** is called a **Range**. You can **Format** more than one **Cell** at the same time by selecting a **Range**.*

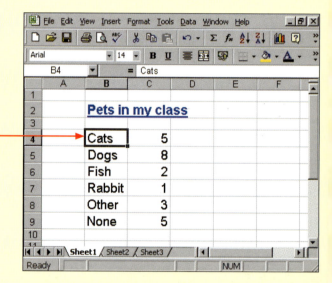

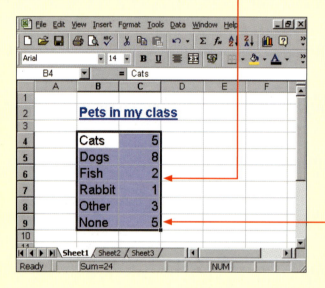

4 Release the mouse button on the last **Cell** in the **Range**.

Selecting Non-adjacent Ranges

5 Select the first **Range**. (**Cells** B4 to C9)

6 Hold down the **Control** key and drag the mouse across the non-adjacent **Range**. (**Cells** E4 to F6)

7 Release the mouse button and the **Control** key on the last **Cell** in the non-adjacent **Range**.

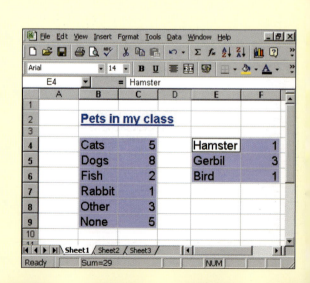

ExcelWorks

1 Open a **New** workbook.

2 Enter the following shopping list into your workbook in **Font Size 10**.

	A	B	C	D	E
1					
2		My Shopping List			
3					
4					
5					
6		Eggs		Lamb	
7		Butter		Beef	
8		Tea		Potatoes	
9		Coffee		Apples	
10		Chicken		Pears	
11		Fish		Carrots	
12					

3 Change the **Font Size** and the **Font Style** of the title.

4 Select both **Ranges** and change the **Font** to **Tahoma**. (See 5a and 3a)

	A	B	C	D	E	F
1						
2		My Shopping List				
3						
4						
5						
6		Eggs		Lamb		
7		Butter		Beef		
8		Tea		Potatoes		
9		Coffee		Apples		
10		Chicken		Pears		
11		Fish		Carrots		
12						

5 Change the **Font Size** to **16**.

6 Change the **Font colour** to **blue**.

7 **Save** your work.

8 **Print** your work.

Sorting into Ascending Order

1 Type a list and select the **Range** that you want to **Sort**. (See 5a)

2 Click **Data**.

3 Click **Sort**.

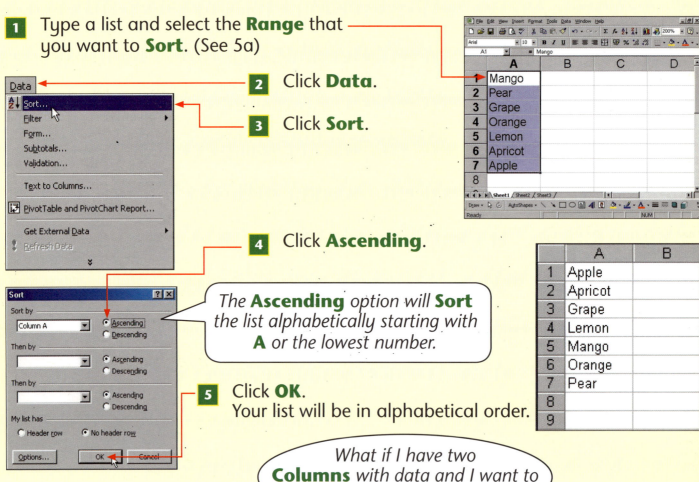

4 Click **Ascending**.

*The **Ascending** option will **Sort** the list alphabetically starting with **A** or the lowest number.*

5 Click **OK**.
Your list will be in alphabetical order.

*What if I have two **Columns** with data and I want to **Sort** only one **Column**?*

- Select the **Column** that you want to **Sort**. Go back to **2**.

- A **Sort Warning** box will appear.

- Click **Continue with the current selection**.

- Click **Sort**.

- Go back to **4**.

*Only **Column A** will be sorted alphabetically. **Column B** will stay the same.*

ExcelWorks

1 **Open** your 'Class List' File.

2 Select a **Range** that includes the names, addresses and shoe sizes. (See 5a) Do not include your name and class.

3 **Sort Column A** in **Ascending** order. (See 6a)

4 **Save** and **Print**.

	A	B	C	D	E	F
1	Ivor Longarm					6
2	Class Y					
3						
4	Penny Lane	100 Whitehart Lane				2
5	Greta Overmann	27 Kings Street				2
6	Jade Bamber	29 Victoria Lane				2
7	Mel Radcliff	576 Liverpool Road				3
8	Katherine Green	99 Mayfair Street				3
9	Bradley Metcalf	89 Cross Roads				3
10	Ibraheem Batan	23 Lane Ends				4
11	Firdaus Patel	56 Fisher Lane				4
12	Harrison Patrick	8 Capital Road				4
13	Antony Blake	2 Elland Road				5
14	Ethan Miles	44 St Georges Way				5
15	Jake Adam	15 Deepdale Road				6
16	Leroy Wayne	73 Riverside				7
17						

5 Look at the letter of the **Column** containing the shoe sizes.

6 Select the same **Range** and **Sort** the shoe sizes **Column** into **Ascending** order.

7 **Save** and **Print**.

8 Now **Sort** the list by name again but use the icon at the top of the screen.

Sort Ascending

Remember

*If you don't select all the **Columns**, only the **Column** that you select will be sorted. You could mix up all the names and addresses if you forget to select all the **Columns**.*

Sorting into Descending Order

> **Descending** order **Sorts** numbers from the highest to the lowest. It **Sorts** letters into reverse alphabetical order, starting with **Z**.

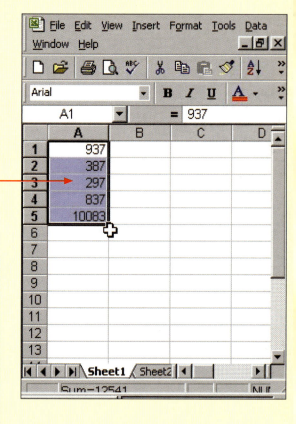

1 Type a list of numbers and select the **Range** you want to **Sort**.

2 Click **Data**.

3 Click **Sort**.

4 Click **Descending**.

5 Click **OK**. Your list will be sorted from highest to lowest.

	A	
1	10083	highest
2	937	
3	837	
4	387	
5	297	lowest
6		

ExcelWorks

1 Open a **New** workbook.

2 Enter the following numbers into your workbook. (See 4a)

	A
1	52
2	66
3	12
4	99
5	108
6	42
7	31
8	24
9	79
10	86
11	

3 Select the **Range** and **Sort** in **Ascending** order. (See 6a)

4 **Save** and **Print**.

5 Now **Sort** in **Descending** order. (See 7a)

6 **Save** and **Print**.

7 Open another **New** workbook.

8 Enter the following animals into your workbook.

	A
1	Parrot
2	Dog
3	Goldfish
4	Hamster
5	Cat
6	Gerbil
7	Budgie
8	Rabbit
9	Snake
10	Tarantula
11	

9 Select the **Range** and **Sort** in **Ascending** order, but use the icons at the top of the screen.

Sort Ascending

Sort Descending

10 **Save** and **Print**.

11 Now **Sort** in **Descending** order.

12 **Save** and **Print**.

Creating a Series

A **Series** is a list that is used often. The standard **Series** in *Excel* include days of the week, months of the year and dates. You need not type every item in a **Series**. *Excel* can create a **Series** automatically.

1 Open a **New** workbook.

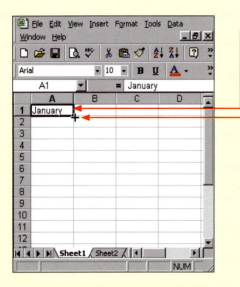

2 Type the first item of your **Series**.

3 Point at the small black box in the right-hand corner of the selected **Cell**. This is called the **Fill handle**. The mouse pointer changes to a cross. ✛

4 Click, hold and drag across or down the **Cells** where you want your **Series** to appear.

5 Release the mouse when you have finished.

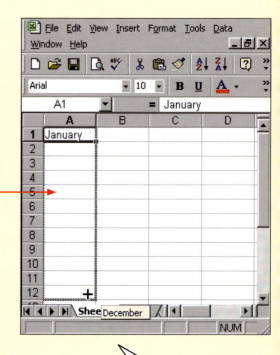

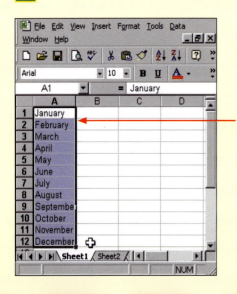

The **Series** will now be filled automatically.

This will save you time, because you do not need to type all the data.

Excel/Works

Create a Class Rota

SKILL: Creating a Series

1 Open a **New** workbook.

2 Create the following **Series** using the **Fill handle** for a weekly rota. (See 8a)

> **Remember**
> Only type in the first **Cell** in your **Series**.

	A	B	C	D	E	F
1		Monday	Tuesday	Wednesday	Thursday	Friday
2	Week 1					
3	Week 2					
4	Week 3					
5	Week 4					
6	Week 5					

The rota shows who is responsible for keeping the classroom tidy each day.

3 Fill in your rota.

4 Change the **Font**, **Font style** and **Font colour** of your rota.

Keep our class tidy

	A	B	C	D	E	F	
1		Monday	Tuesday	Wednesday	Thursday	Friday	
2	Week 1	John	Penny	Luke	Jeni	Mark	
3	Week 2	Chris	George	Kirsty	Richard	Fatima	
4	Week 3	Raj	Yusra	Jake	Harriet	Daniel D	
5	Week 4	Jasmine	Daniel R	Brooke	Leon	William	
6	Week 5	Becky	David	Samantha	Andrew	Nicki	
7							

5 **Save** and **Print**.

6 Create a rota to show who washes up each day in your home.

*What if I filled in too many **Cells**?*

- Select the **Range** containing the **Series**.

- Click the **Fill handle** and drag backwards to remove the unwanted **Cells**.

ExcelWorks

Using Print Preview

9a SKILL

Print Preview lets you look at your work before you **Print** it.

1 **Open** an existing workbook.

2 Click **File**.

3 Click **Print Preview**.

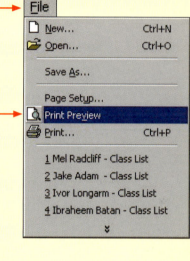

File
New...	Ctrl+N
Open...	Ctrl+O
Save As...	
Page Setup...	
Print Preview	
Print...	Ctrl+P
1 Mel Radcliff - Class List	
2 Jake Adam - Class List	
3 Ivor Longarm - Class List	
4 Ibraheem Batan - Class List	

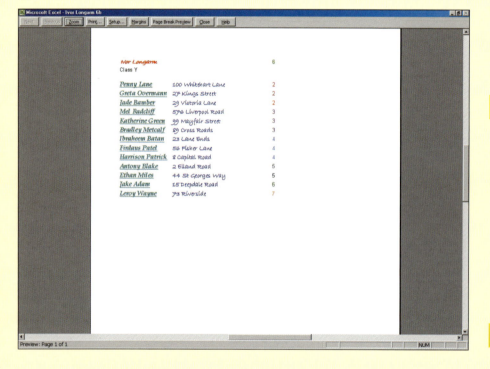

4 If you want to change something:

● Click **Close**.

● Make your changes.

● **Print Preview**.
(Go back to **3**)

5 When you are happy with the page, **Save** and **Print**.

Remember
The gridlines from your workbook will not show in **Print** *Preview* *if your computer is not set up to* **Print** *them.*

Make a Record of Attendance

9b

SKILL: Using Print Preview

APPLICATION

1 Copy the following data using the **Fill handle**. (See 8a)

	A	B
1		Attendance for 4 weeks
2		
3		Week 1
4		
5		Monday
6		Tuesday
7		Wednesday
8		Thursday
9		Friday

2 Complete the table with your class attendance.

3 Change the **Font**, **Font style** and **Font colour** of the table contents.

4 Use **Print Preview** to check that you are happy with your work. (See 9a)

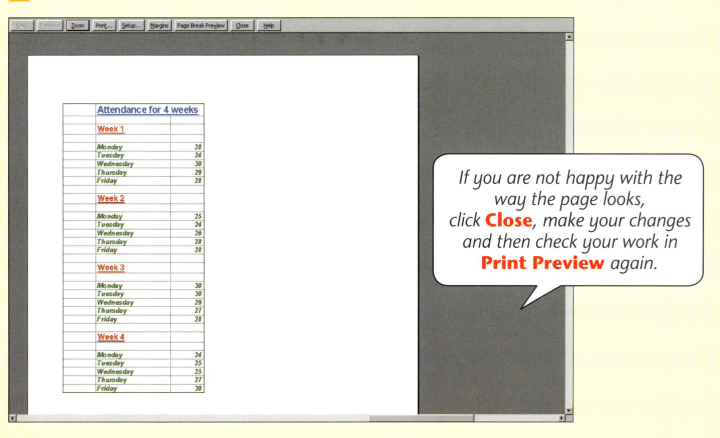

*If you are not happy with the way the page looks, click **Close**, make your changes and then check your work in **Print Preview** again.*

5 **Save** and **Print**.

Setting Up a Landscape Page

SKILL 10a

A **Portrait** page gives you more depth.
A **Landscape** page gives you more width.

If your work will not fit on one page because there are too many **Columns**, set the page to **Landscape**.

| Portrait | Landscape |

1 Click **File**.

2 Click **Page Setup**.

3 Click the **Page** tab.

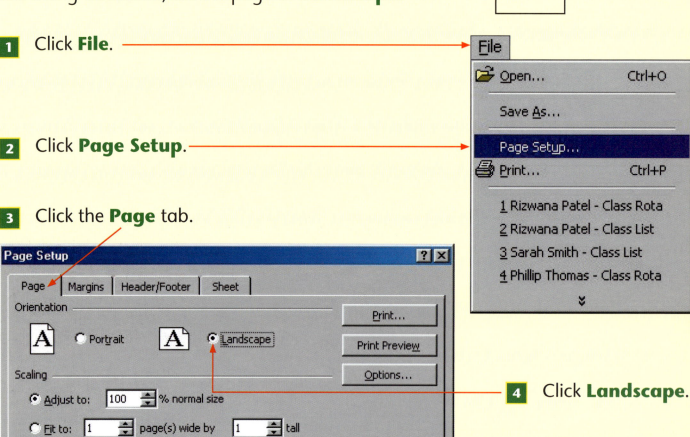

4 Click **Landscape**.

5 Click **OK**.

The page will now be set to **Landscape**.

Days in Each Month

10b

APPLICATION

1 Open a **New** workbook.

2 Enter the following table using the **Fill handle**. (See 8a)

	A	B	C	D	E	F	G	H	I	J	K	L
1			Table to show the number of days in each month									
2												
3	January	February	March	April	May	June	July	August	September	October	November	December

3 Fill in the number of days in each month in the **Row** below.

4 Click **Print Preview** to see if the table fits on one page. (See 9a)

5 Set your page to **Landscape**. (See 10a)

6 Click **Print Preview** to check the table again.

7 **Save** and **Print**.

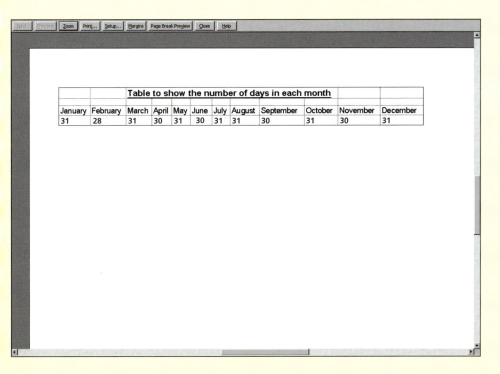

*What if I want my numbers to appear in the centre of each **Cell**?*

- Click the number of the **Row**. This will select the whole **Row**.

- Click the **Center** (**Centre**) icon

Center

Before entering data, you can select the number of **Decimal places** you want.

	A	B
1	1.23	2 decimal places
2	2.365	3 decimal places
3	21.5497	4 decimal places

1 Click **Format**.

2 Click **Cells**.

3 Click the **Number** tab.

4 Click **Number**.

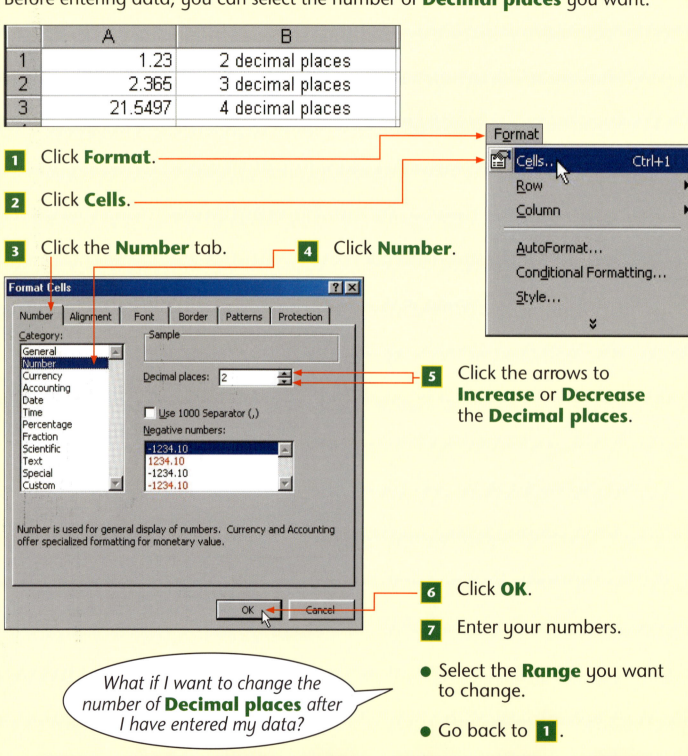

5 Click the arrows to **Increase** or **Decrease** the **Decimal places**.

6 Click **OK**.

7 Enter your numbers.

*What if I want to change the number of **Decimal places** after I have entered my data?*

● Select the **Range** you want to change.

● Go back to **1**.

1   Open a **New** workbook.

2   Copy the following table.

	A	B	C	D	E
1					
2		mm	cm	m	km
3		1	0.1		
4		2			
5		5			
6		10			
7		20			
8		30			
9					

3   Enter all the numbers in the **cm Column** and select the appropriate number of **Decimal places**. (See 11a)

4   Enter all the numbers in the **m Column** and select the appropriate number of **Decimal places**.

5   Enter all the numbers in the **km Column** and select the appropriate number of **Decimal places.** This time, use the icons at the top of the screen.

Increase Decimal

Decrease Decimal

6   **Save** and **Print**.

Using Currency

1 Select the **Cells** to which you wish to add a currency symbol.

2 Click **Format**.

3 Click **Cells**.

4 Click the **Number** tab.　　**5** Click **Currency**.

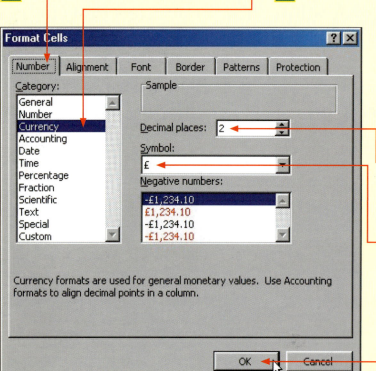

6 Check the number of **Decimal places** is set to **2**. (See 11a)

7 Check the **Symbol** is correct, for example **£**.

8 Click **OK**.

9 Enter your money values.

	A
1	£50.00
2	£0.50
3	£9.34
4	
5	
6	

What if the amount is less than £1?

● If the amount is in pence, for example 50p, then enter 0.50

Add Prices to a Shopping List

SKILL: Using Currency

12b

APPLICATION

1 **Open** the File in which you saved your 'Shopping List' work. (See 5b)

2 Enter the price of each item. (See 12a)

	A	B	C	D	E	F
1						
2		My Shopping List				
3						
4						
5						
6		Eggs	£ 1.20	Lamb	£4.20	
7		Butter	£ 0.98	Beef	£2.20	
8		Tea	£ 3.99	Potatoes	£1.32	
9		Coffee	£ 1.80	Apples	£0.56	
10		Chicken	£ 4.99	Pears	£0.64	
11		Fish	£ 1.50	Carrots	£0.78	
12						
13						

Remember
Use the full stop for a decimal point.

3 **Save** and **Print**.

*What if I forgot to add the **Currency Symbol** before I entered the prices?*

	A	B	C	D	E	F
1						
2		My Shopping List				
3						
4						
5						
6		Eggs	£ 1.20	Lamb	£4.20	
7		Butter	£ 0.98	Beef	£2.20	
8		Tea	£ 3.99	Potatoes	£1.32	
9		Coffee	£ 1.80	Apples	£0.56	
10		Chicken	£ 4.99	Pears	£0.64	
11		Fish	£ 1.50	Carrots	£0.78	
12						

- Select all the prices in a **Non-adjacent Range**.

- Go to **Format – Cells** and select the **Currency** symbol.

Remember
*You can also select the prices then click the **Currency** icon.*

Currency

ExcelWorks

Changing the Column Width Size

1 Click the letter at the top of the **Column** whose **Width** you want to change.

2 Click **Format**.

3 Move to **Column**.

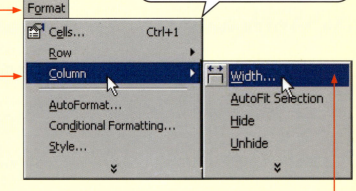

> Your workbook will open with equal-sized **Column Widths** (of 8.43).

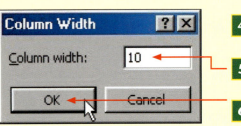

4 Click **Width**.

5 Enter a new **Column Width** size.

6 Click **OK**. The **Column Width** will now be changed.

Using AutoFit to change the Column Width

> If the text I type does not fit into a **Cell**, I can change the **Width** of the **Column**.

7 Move the mouse to the top right corner of the **Column**, next to the letter, until the pointer has changed to: ↔

8 Double-click the mouse. Your **Column Width** will resize automatically to make the **Column** fit the text.

> You can also use **Format Menu** to use **AutoFit**. Select the **Column**. Click **Format** then move to **Column** and then click **AutoFit Selection**.

	A	B	C
1	I have used AutoFit to change the column width.		

Adjust the Column Widths of your Class List

SKILL: Changing Column Width

13b

APPLICATION

1 **Open** the workbook in which you saved your 'Class List'. (See 6b)

2 Change the **Column Width** for the addresses **Column**.
Use the 'Changing the Column width size' method. (See 13a)

3 Change the **Column Width** for the shoe sizes **Column**.
Use **AutoFit** by double-clicking the top corner of the **Column** next to the letter.

	A	B	C	D	E	F	G
1	Ivor Longarm					6	
2	Class Y						
3							
4	Penny Lane		100 Whitehart Lane			2	
5	Greta Overmann		27 Kings Street			2	
6	Jade Bamber		29 Victoria Lane			2	
7	Mel Radcliff		576 Liverpool Road			3	
8	Katherine Green		99 Mayfair Street			3	
9	Bradley Metcalf		89 Cross Roads			3	
10	Ibraheem Batan		23 Lane Ends			4	
11	Firdaus Patel		56 Fisher Lane			4	
12	Harrison Patrick		8 Capital Road			4	
13	Antony Blake		2 Elland Road			5	
14	Ethan Miles		44 St Georges Way			5	
15	Jake Adam		15 Deepdale Road			6	
16	Leroy Wayne		73 Riverside			7	
17							

This is the **Separator Line**.

	A	B
1		
2		

4 **Save** and **Print**.

*You can also change the **Column Width** by putting the cursor on the **Separator Line**. When the cursor changes to ↔, drag the **Separator Line** to the **Column Width** you want, then release the mouse.*

ExcelWorks

Changing the Height of Rows

Entering the Row Height Size

1 Click the number of the **Row** whose height you want to change.

2 Click **Format**.

3 Move to **Row**.

*Your workbook will open with equal-sized **Row Heights** (of 12.75).*

Format

Cells...	Ctrl+1	
Row	▶	Height...
Column	▶	AutoFit
AutoFormat...		Hide
Conditional Formatting...		Unhide
Style...		
⋁		

4 Click **Height**.

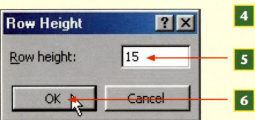

Row Height

Row height: 15

OK   Cancel

5 Enter a new **Row Height** size.

6 Click **OK**. Your **Row Height** will now be changed.

Using AutoFit to change the Row Height

*You can change the **Row Height** to make the data easier to read and to make a table look more attractive.*

7 Move the mouse to the bottom of a **Row**, next to the number, until the pointer has changed to: ↕

8 Double-click the mouse. Your **Row Height** will resize automatically to make the text fit.

*You can also use **Format Menu** to use **AutoFit**. Select the **Row**. Click **Format** then move to **Row** and then click **AutoFit Selection**.*

Adjust the Row Heights of your Class List

SKILL: Changing Row Heights

14b

APPLICATION

1 **Open** the workbook in which you saved your 'Class List'. (See 13b)

2 Select a **Range** including all the names, addresses and shoe sizes beneath your class name and change the **Row Height** to **25**. (See 14a)

3 Select the **Range** again and change the **Font Size** to **16**.

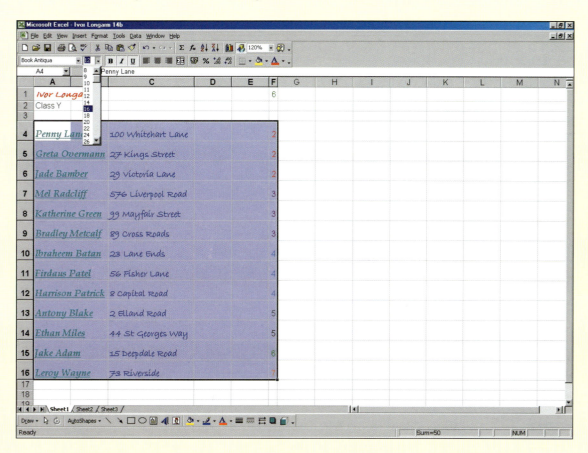

4 Check your work in **Print Preview** – you may need to set your page to **Landscape**. (See 9a and 10a)

*You can also change the **Row Height** by putting the cursor on the **Separator Line**. When the cursor changes to ↔, drag the **Separator Line** to the **Row Height** you want, then release the mouse.*

5 **Save** and **Print**.

Inserting Columns and Rows

15a SKILL

Inserting Columns

A new **Column** is always inserted to the left of the **Column** you have selected. For example, if you type text in **Cell C1** and you **Insert** a new **Column**, your text will be moved to **Cell D1** as the new **Column** is inserted to the left.

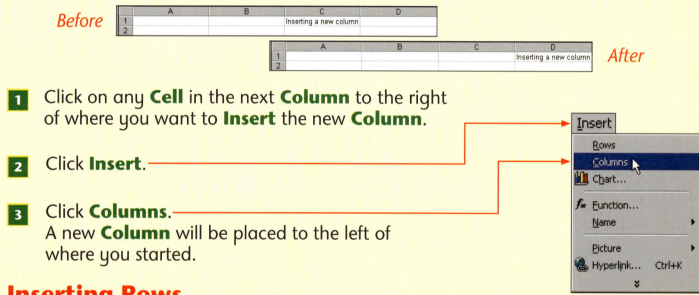

Before

After

1 Click on any **Cell** in the next **Column** to the right of where you want to **Insert** the new **Column**.

2 Click **Insert**.

3 Click **Columns**.
A new **Column** will be placed to the left of where you started.

Inserting Rows

A new **Row** is always inserted above the **Row** you have selected. For example, if you type text in **Cell B3** and you **Insert** a new **Row**, your text will be moved to **Cell B4** as the new **Row** is inserted above.

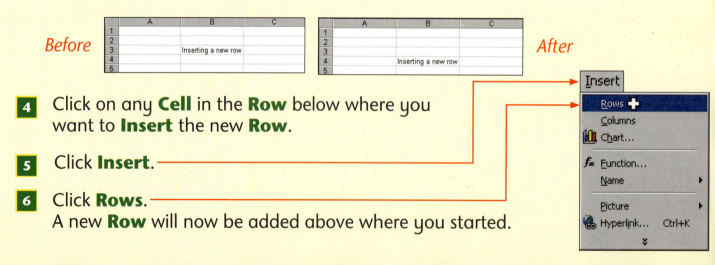

Before

After

4 Click on any **Cell** in the **Row** below where you want to **Insert** the new **Row**.

5 Click **Insert**.

6 Click **Rows**.
A new **Row** will now be added above where you started.

Add Columns and Rows to your Class List

SKILL: Inserting Columns and Rows

15b

APPLICATION

1 **Open** the workbook in which you saved your 'Class List'. (See 14b)

2 **Insert** a new **Column** between the address and the shoe sizes **Columns**. (See 15a)

3 Add the telephone number of each person on your list in the new **Column**.

	A	B	C	D	E	F	G	H
1	Ivor Longarm						6	
2	Class Y							
3								
4	Penny Lane		100 Whitehart Lane	741813			2	
5	Greta Overmann		27 Kings Street	700615			2	
6	Jade Bamber		29 Victoria Lane				2	
7	Mel Radcliff		576 Liverpool Road				3	
8	Katherine Green		99 Mayfair Street				3	
9	Bradley Metcalf		89 Cross Roads				4	
10	Ibraheem Batan		23 Lane Ends				4	
11	Firdaus Patel		56 Fisher Lane				4	
12	Harrison Patrick		8 Capital Road				4	
13	Antony Blake		2 Elland Road				5	
14	Ethan Miles		44 St Georges Way				5	
15	Jake Adam		15 Deepdale Road				6	
16	Leroy Wayne		73 Riverside				7	
17								

4 **Insert** a **Row** above the first name.

	A	B	C	D	E	F	G	H
1	Ivor Longarm						6	
2	Class Y							
3								
4	**Name**		**Address**	**Telephone Number**			**Shoe Size**	
5	Penny Lane		100 Whitehart Lane	741813			2	
6	Greta Overmann		27 Kings Street	700615			2	
7	Jade Bamber		29 Victoria Lane	815254			2	
8	Mel Radcliff		576 Liverpool Road	765215			3	

5 Add **Column** headings and **Centre** them using the **Center** (**Centre**) icon.

Center

6 **Save** and **Print**.

16a SKILL

Deleting Columns and Rows

Deleting Columns

1 Click any **Cell** in the **Column** that you want to **Delete**.

2 Click **Edit**.

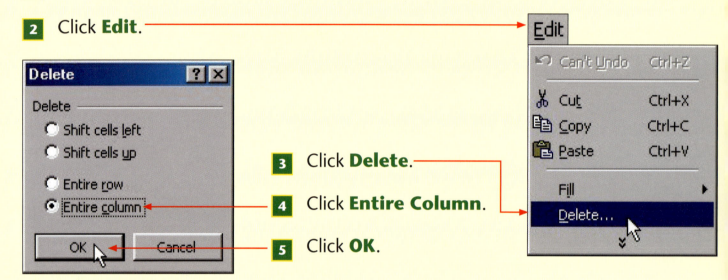

3 Click **Delete**.

4 Click **Entire Column**.

5 Click **OK**.

Deleting Rows

6 Click any **Cell** in the **Row** that you want to **Delete**.

7 Click **Edit**.

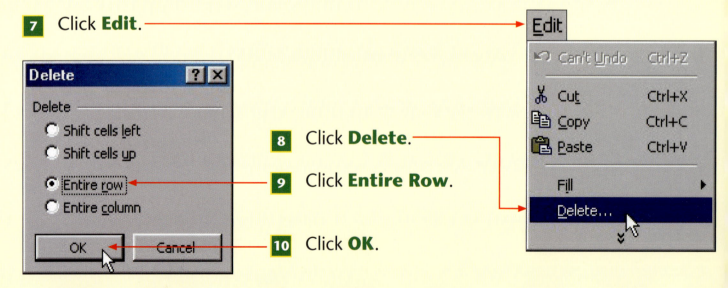

8 Click **Delete**.

9 Click **Entire Row**.

10 Click **OK**.

Change a Worksheet

SKILL: Deleting Columns and Rows

16b

APPLICATION

1 Open the workbook in which you saved your 'Class List'. (See 15b)

	A	B	C	D	E	F	G
1	Ivor Longarm						6
2	Class Y						
3							
4	**Name**		**Address**	**Telephone Number**			**Shoe Size**
5	Penny Lane		100 Whitehart Lane	741813			2
6	Greta Overmann		27 Kings Street	700615			2
7	Jade Bamber		29 Victoria Lane	815254			2
8	Mel Radcliff		576 Liverpool Road	765215			3

2 **Delete** the **Column** that contains the telephone numbers of your classmates. (See 16a)

	A	B	C	D	E	F	G
1	Ivor Longarm					6	
2	Class Y						
3							
4	**Name**		**Address**		**Shoe Size**		
5	Penny Lane		100 Whitehart Lane		2		
6	Greta Overmann		27 Kings Street		2		
7	Jade Bamber		29 Victoria Lane		2		
8	Mel Radcliff		576 Liverpool Road		3		

3 **Delete** a member of your class and their details.

	A	B	C	D	E	F	G
1	Ivor Longarm					6	
2	Class Y						
3							
4	**Name**		**Address**		**Shoe Size**		
5	Penny Lane		100 Whitehart Lane		2		
6	Jade Bamber		29 Victoria Lane		2		
7	Mel Radcliff		576 Liverpool Road		3		
8	Bradley Metcalf		89 Cross Roads		3		

4 **Save** and **Print**.

If you type a lot of text into a **Cell**, the **Cell** expands and runs over other **Cells** unless you **Wrap text**.

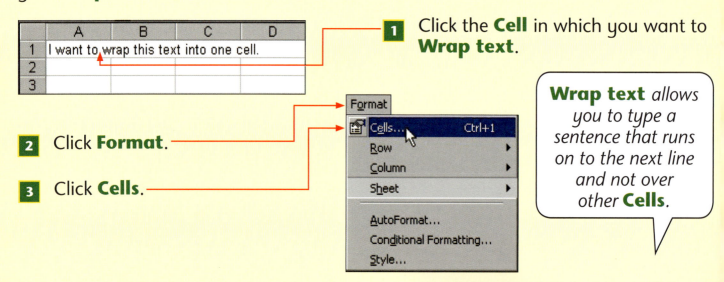

1 Click the **Cell** in which you want to **Wrap text**.

2 Click **Format**.

3 Click **Cells**.

Wrap text allows you to type a sentence that runs on to the next line and not over other **Cells**.

4 Click the **Alignment** tab.

5 Click **Wrap text**.

6 Click **OK**.

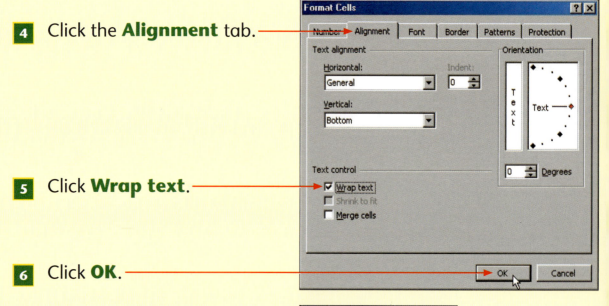

Your text will now be wrapped in one **Cell**.

Make Text Fit into Cells

SKILL: Wrapping Text

17b

APPLICATION

1 Open a **New** workbook.

2 Type 'First Name' in **Cell A3**.

3 Type 'Surname' in **Cell A4**.

4 Type 'Height in Centimetres' in **Cell A5**.

> *You have to click the **Cell** in which you want to **Wrap text** before you click **Format**.*

5 Type 'Weight in Kilograms' in **Cell A6**.

6 **Wrap** the **text** in **Cell A5** and **Cell A6**. (See 17a)

7 Fill in the information for five members of your class.

8 Change the **Font**, **Font style** and **Font colour** of your data – you may need to adjust the widths of **Columns**. (See 13a)

	A	B	C	D	E	F	G
1							
2							
3	First Name	David	Tracy	Matlub	Oliver	Sarah	
4	Surname	Green	Kelly	Member	Lowry	French	
5	Height in Centimetres	123	120	145	132	151	
6	Weight in Kilograms	24	39	41	35	42	
7							
8							

9 **Save** and **Print**.

1 Click the **Cell** that contains the text you want to **Shrink to fit** the **Column Width**.

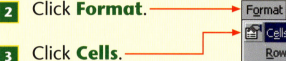

2 Click **Format**.

3 Click **Cells**.

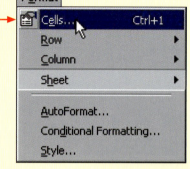

4 Click the **Alignment** tab.

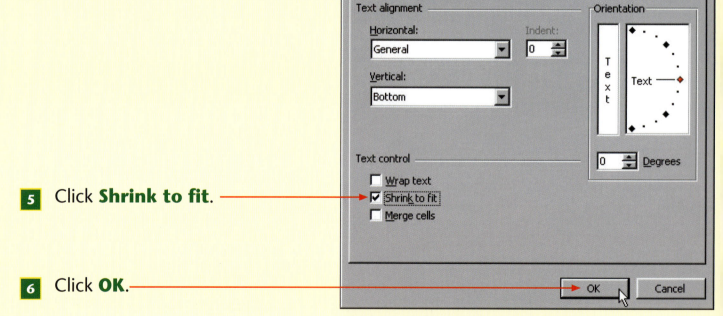

5 Click **Shrink to fit**.

6 Click **OK**.

Your text will now be shrunk to fit the **Column Width**.

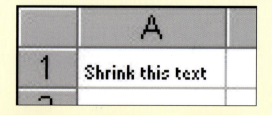

Shrink Text to Fit Cells

SKILL: Shrinking Text

18b

APPLICATION

1 Open a **New** workbook.

2 Enter the following information into the workbook.

	A	B	C	D	E	F	G	H
1	**Temperatures in different locations of the school**							
2								
3								
4	Location	Temperature						
5	My Classroom							
6	Hall							
7	Playground							
8	Stage							
9	Classroom 1							
10	Classroom 2							
11								

3 Enter the temperatures (in °C) of the different locations in your school.

4 Change the **Font colour** of the headings 'Location' and 'Temperature'.

5 **Shrink** the locations so they fit in their **Cells**. (See 18a)

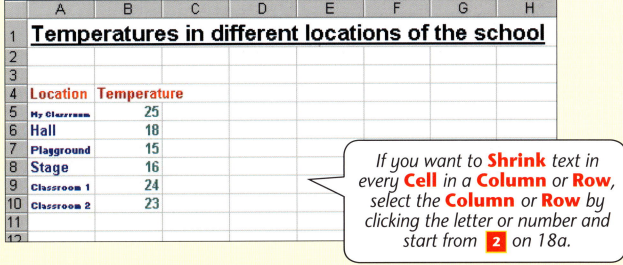

*If you want to **Shrink** text in every **Cell** in a **Column** or **Row**, select the **Column** or **Row** by clicking the letter or number and start from **2** on 18a.*

6 **Save** and **Print**.

19a

SKILL

1. Open a **New** workbook.

2. Find the **Align** icons at the top of your screen. →

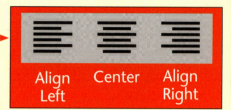

Align Left   Center   Align Right

3. Select a **Cell**.

4. Click the appropriate icon to **Align Left**, **Centre** or **Align Right**.

5. Click the **Column** letter to **Align** the entire **Column**.

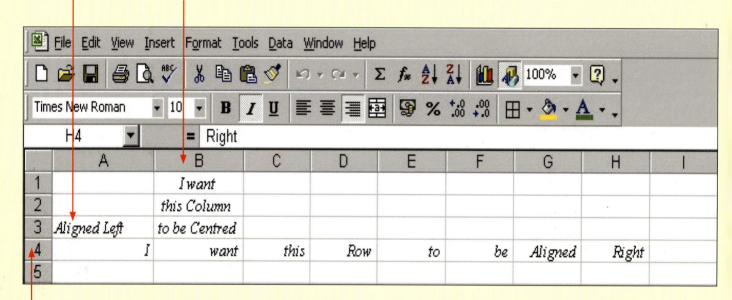

6. Click the **Row** number to **Align** the entire **Row**.

*If you want to **Align** only a few **Cells**, select the **Range**, then click the **Align** icon of your choice.*

Temperature Changes in a Day

SKILL: Aligning

19b

APPLICATION

1 Open a **New** workbook.

2 Enter the following table. You will need to:

- Change the **Font Size** to **12**.

- Change the **Column Widths**. (See 13a)

- **Wrap text**. (See 17a)

3 Record the temperature in your classroom throughout the day.

	A	B	C	D
1	Temperature Changes In A Day			
2				
3		Time	Temperature in Degrees Celsius	
4		09:00	15	
5		10:00	17	
6		11:00	18	
7		12:00	18	
8		13:00	22	
9		14:00	21	
10		15:00	20	
11				

4 Change the **Font styles** and **Font colours**.

5 **Centre** the titles. (See 19a)

6 **Centre** each of the times.

7 **Centre** each of the temperatures.

8 **Save** and **Print**.

	A	B	C
1	Temperature Changes In A Day		
2			
3		Time	Temperature in Degrees Celsius
4		09:00	15
5		10:00	17
6		11:00	18
7		12:00	18
8		13:00	22
9		14:00	21
10		15:00	20
11			

20a
SKILL

Adding Borders to all your data

*The gridlines that are on the screen do not print, so you need to add **Borders**.*

1 Open a **New** workbook.

2 To add **Borders** that cover all the **Active Cells** on your worksheet, click the **Select All** button in the top left-hand corner of the worksheet.

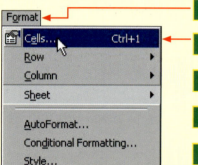

3 Click **Format**.

4 Click **Cells**.

5 Click the **Border** tab.

6 Click **Inside**.

7 Click **OK**.
Your worksheet will now have gridlines around all the data when it is printed.

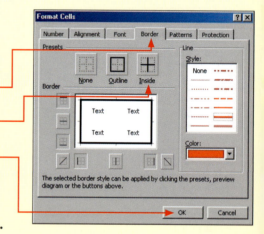

Adding Borders to a single Cell, Row or Column

8 Select the **Cells** to which you want to add a **Border** and follow instructions **3** to **5**.

9 Select the **Border Style** of your choice.

10 Click **OK**.

11 Try adding a **Border Style** to more **Cells** using the icon at the top of your screen.

Borders

*If you want to remove a **Border**.*

● Select the **Cell** or **Range** from which you want to remove the **Borders**. Go back to **3** and when you reach **6** choose the **None** option.

20b

APPLICATION

Find out who has what pets in your class.

Pets	Number of Pets
Dogs	
Cats	
Fish	
Rabbit	
Other type of pet	
No Pets	

1 Open a **New** workbook.

2 Enter the title 'Pets in Our Class'.

3 Add the **Column titles** 'Pets' and 'Number of Pets'.

4 Add to the **Cells**, the information you have collected.

5 Select the **Cells** that contain headings and data, and add a **Border** to them. (See 20a)

6 **Centre** the information in the table. (See 19a)

Center

7 You may want to change the **Font**, **Font Size**, **Font style** and **Font colour**.

8 **Save** and **Print**.

	A	B	C	D
1		Pets in Our Class		
2				
3				
4				
5		Pets	Number of Pets	
6		Dogs	5	
7		Cats	4	
8		Fish	6	
9		Rabbit	1	
10		Other type of pet	2	
11		No Pets	8	
12				
13				

Using Fill

You can add a **Fill Color** (**Colour**) to your **Cells** in two different ways. You can choose a background colour for the **Cells** using the icon.

Fill Color

1 Open a **New** workbook.

*You can add colour to a single **Cell** or to more **Cells** by selecting a **Range** of **Cells**.*

2 Select the **Cells** to which you want to add a background colour.

3 Click the arrow to the right of the **Fill** icon.

4 Click the **Fill Color** (**Colour**) of your choice.

	A	B	C	D
1				
2		I have filled this in pale blue.		
3				

Or you can:

5 Select the **Cells** to which you want to add a background **Colour**.

6 Click **Format**.

7 Click **Cells**.

8 Click the **Patterns** tab.

9 Click a **Fill Color** (**Colour**).

10 **Preview** the colour.

11 Click **OK**.

*What if I decide to remove the **Fill**?*

- Select the **Cells** that you want to remove colour from.
- Go back to **6** and choose the **No Color** (**Colour**) option.

Excel/Works

Add Colour to Tables

SKILL: Using Fill

21b

APPLICATION

1 Enter this table in your workbook and fill in the information according to your class.

	A	B	C	D
1				
2		Favourite Sports		
3				
4		Sport	Number in Class	
5		Tennis		
6		Football		
7		Cricket		
8		Netball		
9		Volleyball		
10				

2 Change the **Font style** and **Font Size** and add **Borders** to the table. (See 20a)

3 Add the corresponding **Fill Colors** (**Colours**) to the **Cells**. (See 21a)

Title – Purple   Sports – Light Green   Number in Class – Yellow

	A	B	C	D
1				
2		**Favourite Sports**		
3				
4		Sport	Number in Class	
5		Tennis	1	
6		Football	15	
7		Cricket	4	
8		Netball	10	
9		Volleyball	0	
10				
11				

4 **Save** and **Print**.

Merging Cells

1 Select the **Cells** that you want to **Merge** into one. For example, **A1** to **F1**.

> *When you **Merge Cells** you combine several **Cells** into one single **Cell**.*

	A	B	C	D	E	F	G
1	Holiday locations						
2							
3	Spain	France	England	USA	Scotland	Tenerife	
4	5	3	10	2	4	5	
5							

2 Click **Format**.

3 Click **Cells**.

Format
	Cells...	Ctrl+1
Row	►
Column	►
Sheet	►
AutoFormat...
Conditional Formatting...
Style...

4 Click the **Alignment** tab.

Format Cells   ? ✕

Number | Alignment | Font | Border | Patterns | Protection

Text alignment
Horizontal:
General ▼   Indent: 0 ⬍

Vertical:
Bottom ▼

Orientation
T e x t   Text ——◆
0 ⬍ Degrees

Text control
☐ Wrap text
☐ Shrink to fit
5 Click **Merge Cells**. → ☑ Merge cells

6 Click **OK**. → OK   Cancel

Your **Cells** will now be merged into one **Cell**.

You can **Centre** the title.

	A	B	C	D	E	F
1	Holiday locations					
2						
3	Spain	France	England	USA	Scotland	Tenerife
4	5	3	10	2	4	5
5						

Temperature Records

SKILL: Merging Cells

22b

APPLICATION

1 Open a **New** workbook.

	A	B	C	D	E
1	Keeping temperature records for a week				
2					
3					
4		Room	Day	Temperature in Degrees C	
5		Class 1	Monday		
6			Tuesday		
7			Wednesday		
8			Thursday		
9			Friday		
10		Class 2	Monday		
11			Tuesday		
12			Wednesday		
13			Thursday		
14			Friday		
15		Class 3	Monday		
16			Tuesday		
17			Wednesday		
18			Thursday		
19			Friday		
20					
21					

2 Enter this table, using the **Fill handle** to create the series of days of the week.

3 Change the **Column Width** to make the **Columns** fit the text.

4 Add your own temperature data or copy the data provided below.

5 **Merge Cells** for the title and each of the classes. (See 22a)

6 **Fill** each merged **Cell** with a different **Fill Color** (**Colour**) and add appropriate **Borders**. (See 21a and 20a)

7 **Save** and **Print**.

	A	B	C	D	E
1		Keeping temperature records for a week			
2					
3					
4		Room	Day	Temperature in Degrees C	
5			Monday	15	
6			Tuesday	16	
7			Wednesday	21	
8			Thursday	18	
9		Class 1	Friday	14	
10			Monday	14	
11			Tuesday	15	
12			Wednesday	21	
13			Thursday	18	
14		Class 2	Friday	16	
15			Monday	16	
16			Tuesday	18	
17			Wednesday	22	
18			Thursday	20	
19		Class 3	Friday	16	
20					

23a

SKILL

Using Merge and Centre

When you **Merge Cells** you combine several **Cells** into one single **Cell**. You can **Centre** the text at the same time.

1 Open a **New** workbook.

2 Select the **Cells** you want to **Merge and Centre**.

3 Click the **Merge and Center** (**Centre**) icon.

Merge and Center

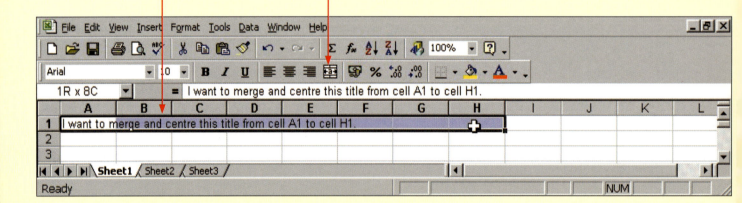

*I can create a title that takes up the width of the worksheet, if I **Merge** the **Cells**.*

	A	B	C	D	E	F	G	H	I
1				I have merged and centred this title from cell A1 to cell H1.					
2									

Remember
*If you have data in the **Cells** you want to **Merge**, only the data in the left-hand **Cell** is kept.*

ExcelWorks

23b

APPLICATION

1 Open a **New** workbook.

2 Enter the following table.

3 Change the **Font Size** of the title to **20**.

	A	B	C	D	E	F
1						
2		Population Density				
3						
4		Country	Density (People per square Km)			
5		Argentina	13			
6		Australia	2			
7		Brazil	20			
8		Cuba	1206			
9		Monaco	30000			
10		UK	241			
11						

4 Change the **Font**, **Font style** and **Font colour** of the table. You might have to change the **Column Widths** of the table.

5 **Centre** the information in the table. (See 19a)

6 Add **Borders** to the table.

7 **Merge and Centre** the title. (See 23a)

	A	B	C
1			
2		Population Density	
3			
4		Country	Density (People per square Km)
5		Argentina	13
6		Australia	2
7		Brazil	20
8		Cuba	1206
9		Monaco	30000
10		UK	241
11			

8 **Save** and **Print**.

Creating Pie Charts

SKILL & APPLICATION

A **Pie Chart** displays the size of each item in relation to the whole.

1 Open the File that you saved your 'Class Pets' table in. (See 20b)

2 Select all the **Cells** that contain information about what the pets are and how many there are.

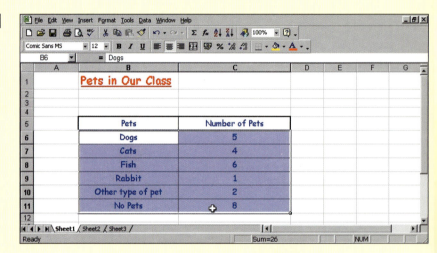

3 Click **Insert**.

4 Click **Chart**.

5 Click the **Standard Types** tab.

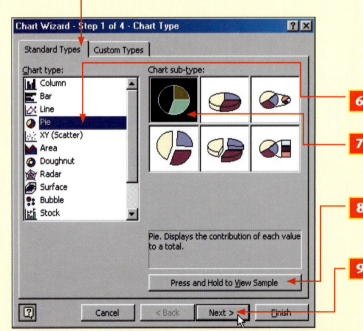

6 Click **Pie** from the **Chart type** list.

7 Click the **Pie Chart sub-type** that you want.

8 Click and hold to **View Sample Chart**.

9 If you are happy with your **Chart**, click **Next**.

(continued on page 51)

Excel*Works*

24

SKILL & APPLICATION

10 View the **Pie Chart**.

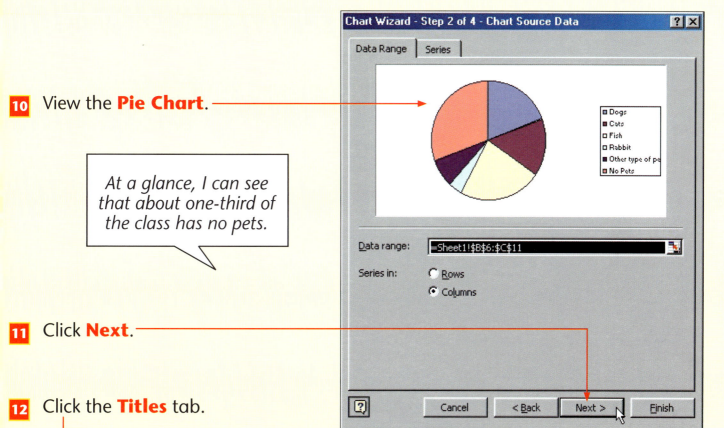

Chart Wizard - Step 2 of 4 - Chart Source Data

Data Range | Series

At a glance, I can see that about one-third of the class has no pets.

Data range: =Sheet1!$B$6:$C$11

Series in: ○ Rows ● Columns

Legend: Dogs, Cats, Fish, Rabbit, Other type of pe, No Pets

11 Click **Next**.

Cancel | < Back | Next > | Finish

12 Click the **Titles** tab.

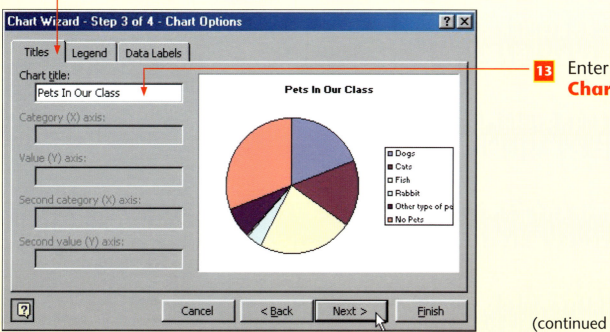

Chart Wizard - Step 3 of 4 - Chart Options

Titles | Legend | Data Labels

Chart title:
Pets In Our Class

Category (X) axis:

Value (Y) axis:

Second category (X) axis:

Second value (Y) axis:

Pets In Our Class

Legend: Dogs, Cats, Fish, Rabbit, Other type of pe, No Pets

Cancel | < Back | Next > | Finish

13 Enter the **Chart Title**.

(continued on page 52)

14 Click the **Data Labels** tab.

15 Select a **Data Label** of your choice.

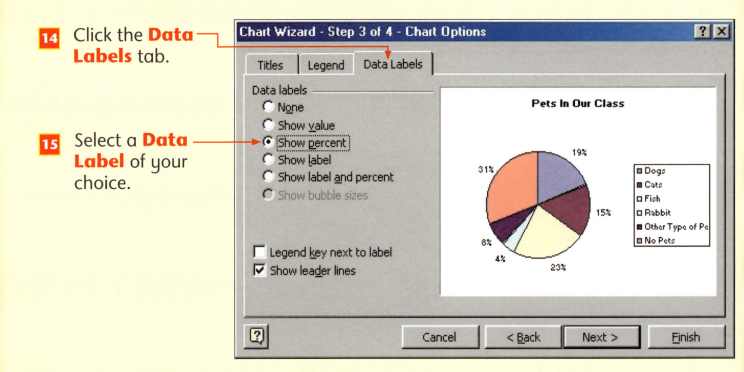

16 Click the **Legend** tab.

*A **Legend** is a key.*

17 Choose a different **Placement** for the **Legend**.

18 Click **Next**.

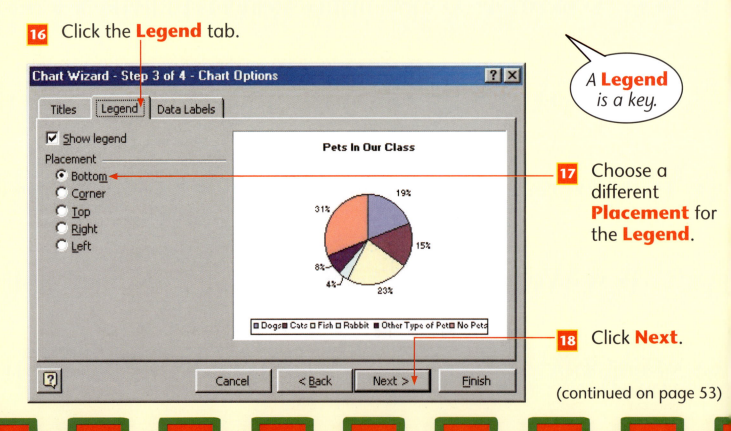

(continued on page 53)

Excel*Works*

24

SKILL & APPLICATION

> *You can put a* **Chart** *on a new sheet or embed a* **Chart** *as an object in an existing sheet.*

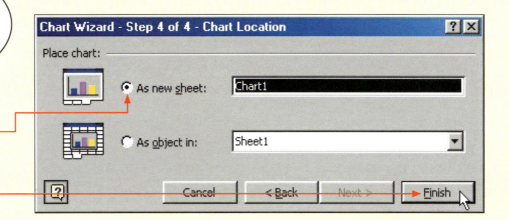

Chart Wizard - Step 4 of 4 - Chart Location

Place chart:

● As new sheet: `Chart1`

○ As object in: `Sheet1`

Cancel   < Back   Next >   Finish

19 Click a **Chart Location**.

20 Click **Finish**. The **Pie Chart** will now be completed.

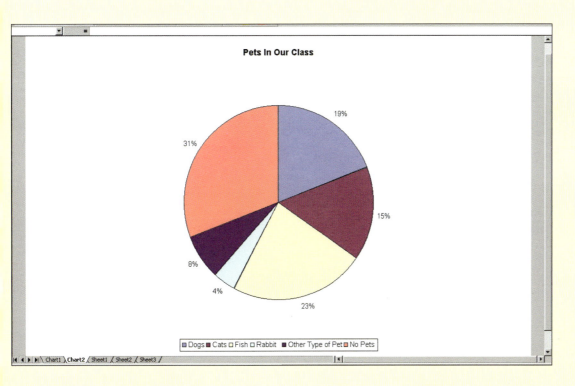

Pets In Our Class

19%
15%
23%
4%
8%
31%

☐ Dogs ☐ Cats ☐ Fish ☐ Rabbit ☐ Other Type of Pet ☐ No Pets

Chart1 \ **Chart2** \ Sheet1 \ Sheet2 \ Sheet3

21 **Save** and **Print**.

22 Try this again by clicking the **Chart Wizard** icon on the toolbar. Try selecting **3D Pie** this time.

Chart Wizard

Creating Column Charts

A **Column Chart** is ideal for showing how data is gathered over time. It allows you to compare items easily.

1 **Open** the File in which you saved your 'Temperature' table, or copy this table.

2 Add **Borders** and change the **Font**, **Font style** and **Font Size** of the text.

	Months	Temperature in Degrees Celsius
	Temperatures In My Town	
	January	4
	February	5
	March	7
	April	9
	May	12
	June	16
	July	18
	August	17
	September	15
	October	11
	November	8
	December	5

3 Select all the **Cells** that contain information about the months and temperatures.

(continued on page 55)

4 Click **Insert**.

5 Click **Chart**.

6 Click the **Standard Types** tab.

7 Click **Column** in the **Chart type** list.

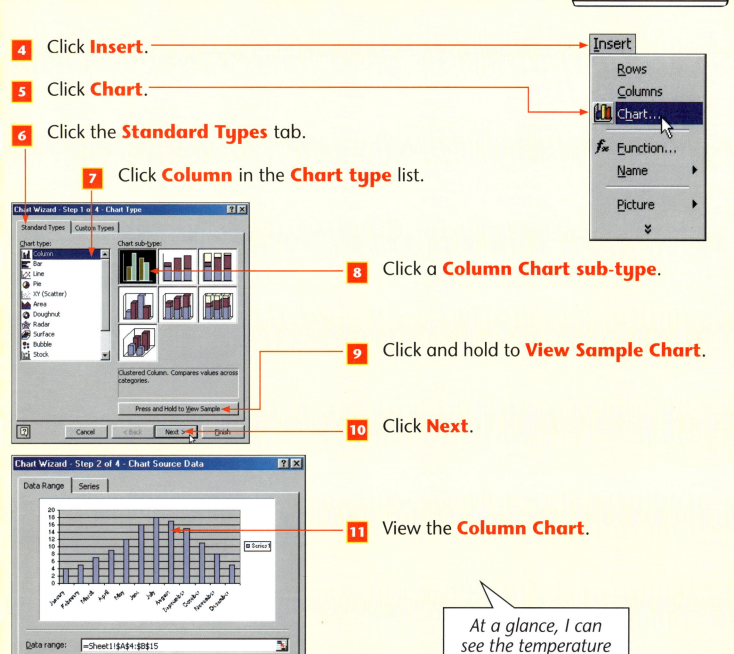

8 Click a **Column Chart sub-type**.

9 Click and hold to **View Sample Chart**.

10 Click **Next**.

11 View the **Column Chart**.

At a glance, I can see the temperature increases each month until July.

12 Click **Next**.

(continued on page 56)

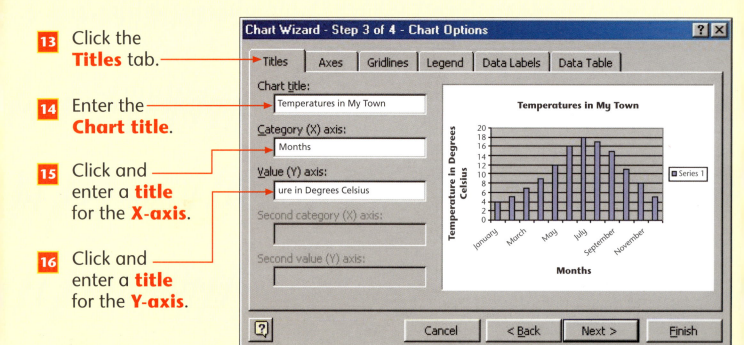

13 Click the **Titles** tab.

14 Enter the **Chart title**.

15 Click and enter a **title** for the **X-axis**.

16 Click and enter a **title** for the **Y-axis**.

*What if I don't want a **Legend**?*

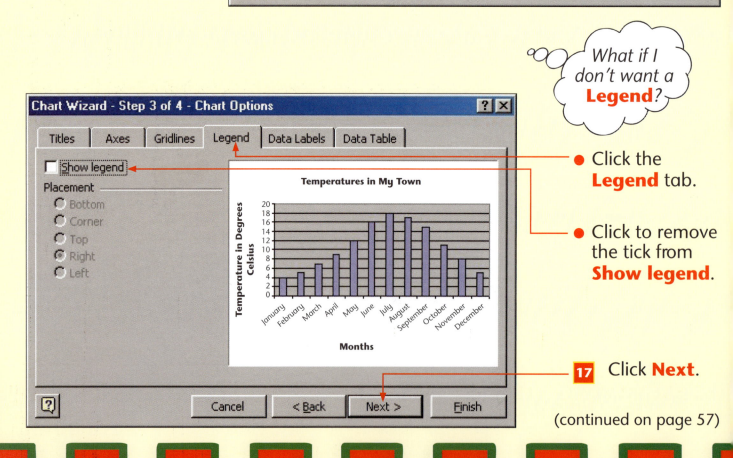

● Click the **Legend** tab.

● Click to remove the tick from **Show legend**.

17 Click **Next**.

(continued on page 57)

*Excel*Works

25

SKILL & APPLICATION

18 Click a **Chart Location**. This will make the **Chart** appear as an object on the worksheet.

19 Click **Finish**. The **Column Chart** will now be completed. The **Chart** will now appear on the worksheet.

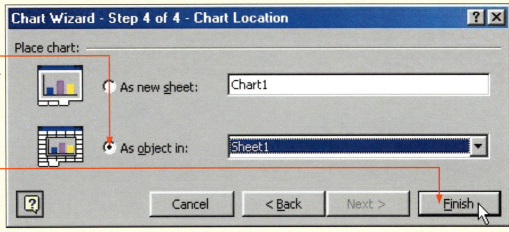

20 Click on the **Chart**.

21 **Save** and **Print**.

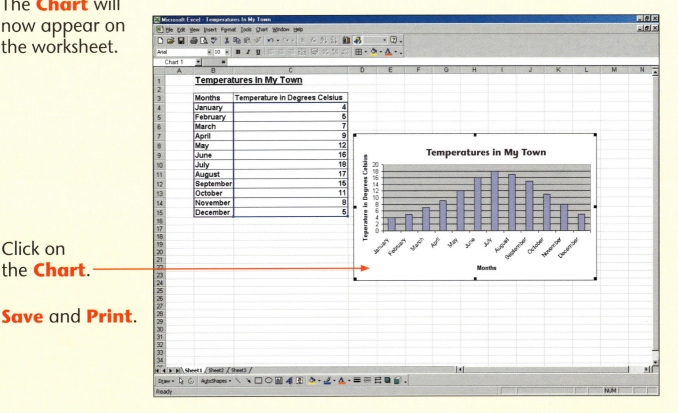

22 Try this again, clicking the **Chart Wizard** icon on the toolbar. Try selecting **3D Column Chart** this time.

Chart Wizard

A **Line Chart** can be used to show the development of data over time.

1 Enter the following table in a **New** workbook.

	A	B	C	D	E	F	G	H	I	J	K	L	M
1													
2	Comparison of Temperatures in Moscow and Hong Kong (in Degrees Celsius)												
3													
4	Months	January	February	March	April	May	June	July	August	September	October	November	December
5	Moscow	-13	-10	-4	6	13	16	18	17	12	6	-1	-7
6	Hong Kong	16	15	18	22	26	28	28	28	27	25	21	18
7													

2 Select all the **Cells** containing information about the months and temperatures.

	A	B	C	D	E	F	G	H	I	J	K	L	M
1													
2	Comparison of Temperatures in Moscow and Hong Kong (in Degrees Celsius)												
3													
4	Months	January	February	March	April	May	June	July	August	September	October	November	December
5	Moscow	-13	-10	-4	6	13	16	18	17	12	6	-1	-7
6	Hong Kong	16	15	18	22	26	28	28	28	27	25	21	18
7													

3 Click **Insert**.

4 Click **Chart**.

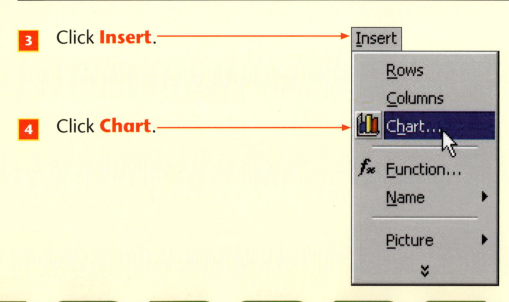

Insert
- Rows
- Columns
- Chart...
- *fx* Function...
- Name ▶
- Picture ▶

(continued on page 59)

26

SKILL & APPLICATION

5 Click the **Standard Types** tab.

6 Click **Line** in the **Chart type** list.

7 Click a **Line Chart sub-type**.

8 Click and hold to **View Sample Chart**.

9 Click **Next**.

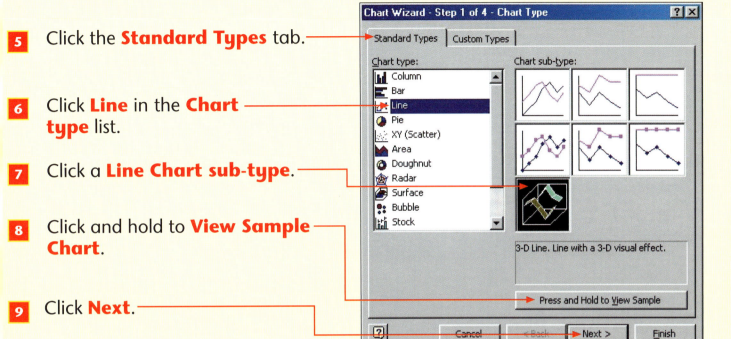

10 View the **Line Chart**.

When you create 3-D Line Charts, you should enter titles for the X and Z axes.

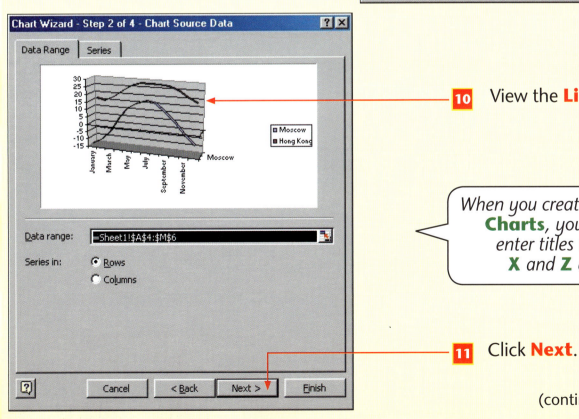

11 Click **Next**.

(continued on page 60)

12 Click the **Titles** tab.

13 Enter the **Chart title**.

14 Click and enter a **title** for the **X-axis**.

15 Click and enter a **title** for the **Z-axis**.

> When you create 2-D **Line Charts**, you should enter titles for the **X** and **Y** axes.

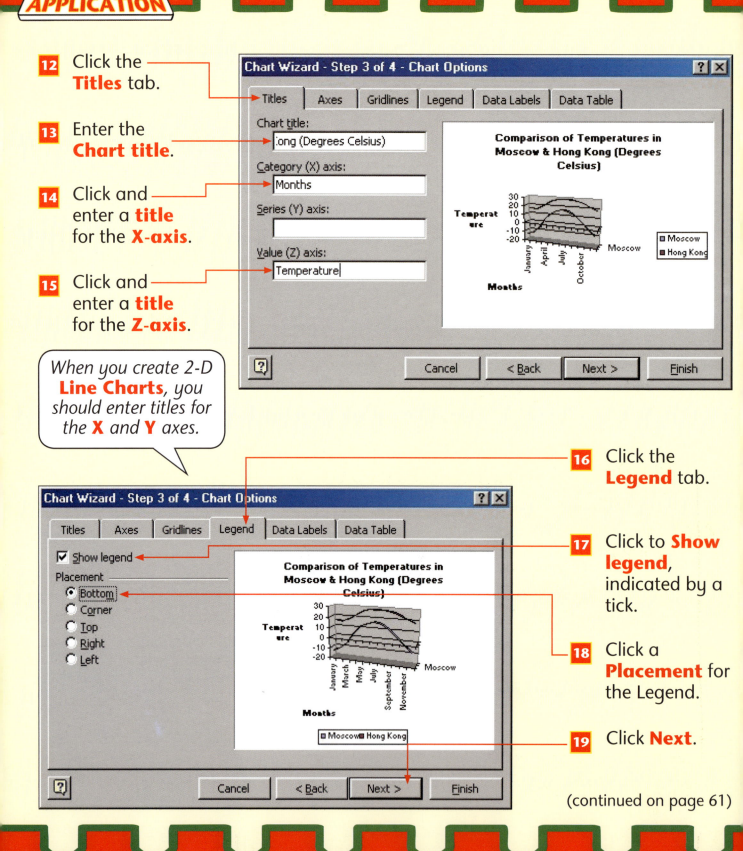

16 Click the **Legend** tab.

17 Click to **Show legend**, indicated by a tick.

18 Click a **Placement** for the Legend.

19 Click **Next**.

(continued on page 61)

SKILL & APPLICATION

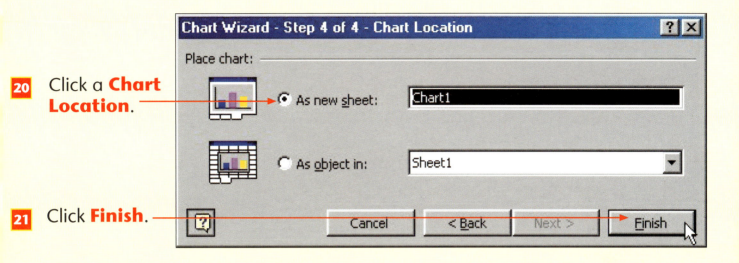

20 Click a **Chart Location**.

21 Click **Finish**.

The **Line Chart** will now be completed.

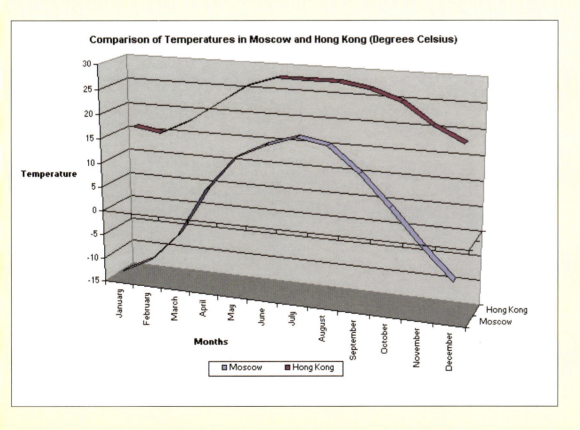

22 **Save** and **Print**.

23 Try this again, clicking the **Chart Wizard** icon on the toolbar.

Chart Wizard

27a SKILL

Moving and Resizing

Moving Charts

1 Open a **Chart** that you have created already.

2 To **Move** the **Chart**, click and drag the **Chart** using the crossed arrows.

3 When it is in the correct place, let go of the mouse.

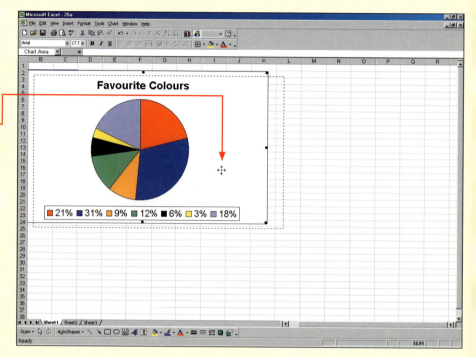

Resizing Charts

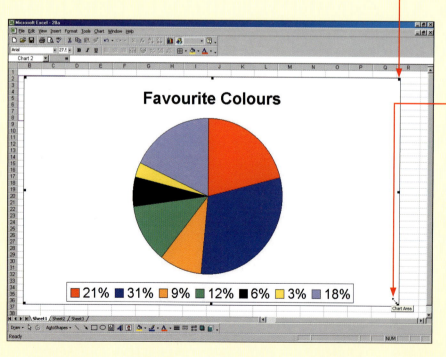

4 Click the white area of the **Chart**, so that you can see small black boxes in the corners.

5 Move the cursor onto one of the boxes around the **Chart**, until it turns into a double-headed arrow.

6 Click and drag the **Chart** to the size that you want.

7 When you are happy with the position and size, click anywhere on the workbook.

1 **Open** the workbook in which you saved your 'Temperatures in My Town' **Column Chart**. (See 25)

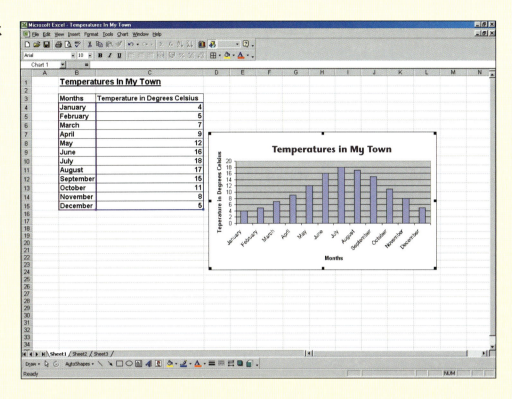

2 **Move** the **Chart**, so that the top left-hand corner is at **A20**. (See 27a)

3 **Resize** the **Chart** by pulling the bottom right-hand corner until you have reached the corner of **H**.

4 **Save** and **Print**.

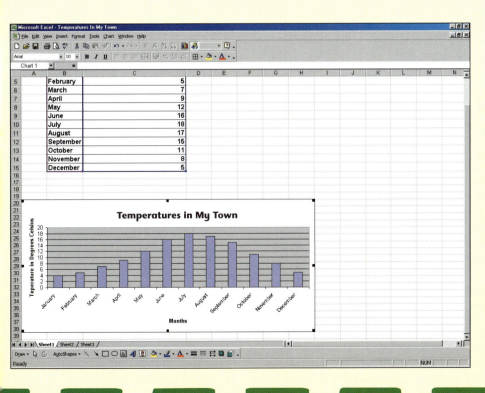

Editing Chart Colours

1 **Open** an existing workbook that contains a **Chart**.

2 Double-click the mouse on the white background. This is the **Chart Area**. The **Format Chart Area** box will open.

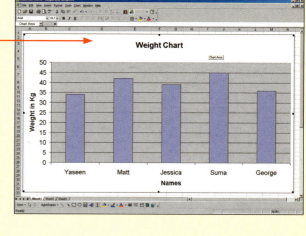

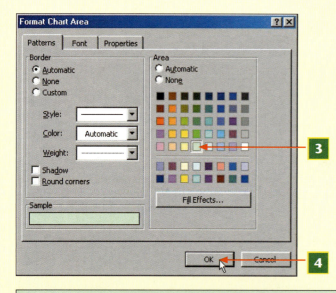

3 Click a **Colour**.

4 Click **OK**.

5 Double-click the background of the graph (the **Plot Area**) to change its **Colour**.

6 Double-click the bars of the graph (the **Data Series**) to change their **Colour**.

7 Try this again by selecting the areas you want to change with a single click and clicking the **Format** icon on the **Chart** toolbar.

To view the toolbar, click **View**, *click* **Toolbar**, *then click* **Chart**.

*Excel*Works

Use Fill Effects

SKILL: Editing Chart Colours

APPLICATION

1 Enter the following table and create a **Column Chart**. (See 25)

2 Select the **Chart Area**. (See 28a)

	A	B
1		
2	Name	Weight in Kg
3	Yaseen	34
4	Matt	42
5	Jessica	39
6	Suma	45
7	George	36
8		

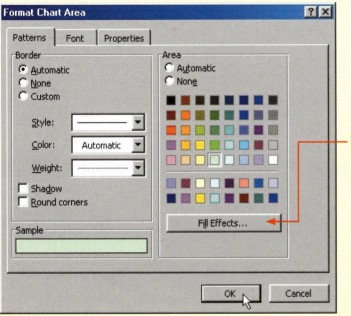

3 Click **Fill Effects**.

4 Click the **Gradient** tab.

5 Click **Preset**.

6 Select a **Preset Color** (**Colour**).

7 Click **OK**.

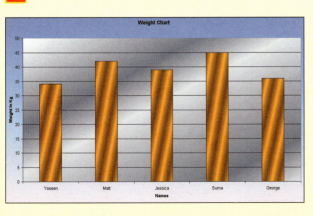

8 Click **OK** in the **Format Chart Area** box. (See 28a)

9 Change the colour of all the areas in the **Chart** using **Fill Effects**.

10 **Save** and **Print**.

29a Changing the Angle of Text

1 **Open** an existing workbook containing a **Chart**.

2 Click to select the text that you want to **Angle**.

3 To **Angle** the text **downwards**, click the **Angle Text Downwards** icon on the **Chart** toolbar.

Your text will now be **Angled downwards**.

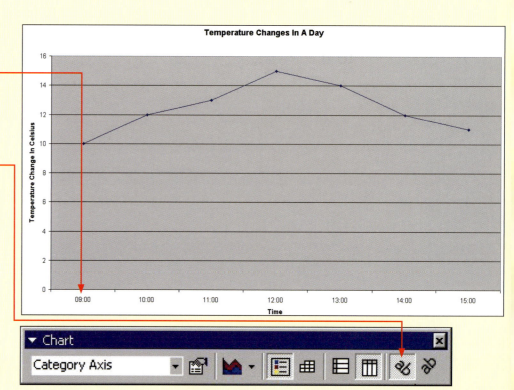

4 To **Angle** the text **upwards**, click the **Angle Text Upwards** icon on the **Chart** toolbar.

Your text will now be **Angled upwards**.

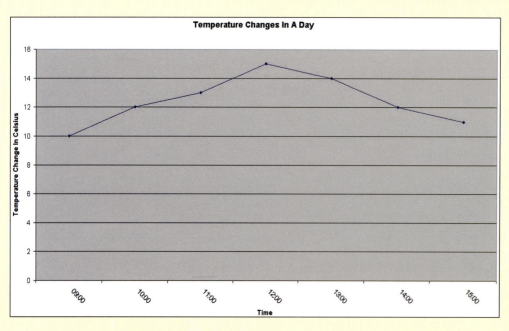

SKILL: Changing the Angle of Text

Country	Population
Argentina	37000000
Bolivia	7500000
Chile	15000000
Colombia	42000000
Ecuador	12500000
Peru	25000000

1 Open a **New** workbook.

2 Add the table opposite.

3 Add **Borders** to the table.

4 Create a **Column Chart** using the table. (See 25)

5 Change the **Colour** of the **Chart Area**. (See 28a)

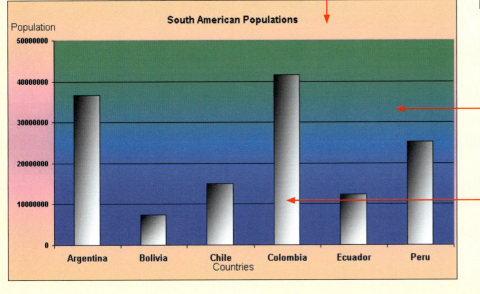

6 Change the **Colour** of the **Plot Area**.

7 Change the **Colour** of the **Data Series**.

8 Change the **Text Angle** on the **Y-axis** to **Upwards**. (See 29a)

9 Change the **Text Angle** on the **X-axis** to **Upwards**.

10 **Save** and **Print**.

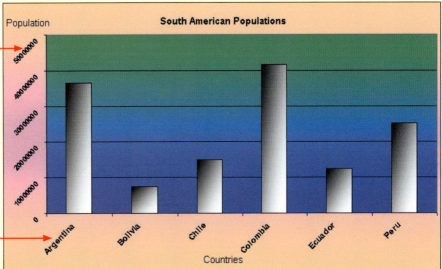

1 **Open** an existing workbook containing a **Chart**.

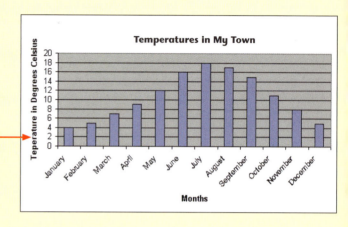

2 Select the **Chart**.

3 Click **Chart**.

4 Click **Chart Type**.

5 Select a new **Chart Type**.

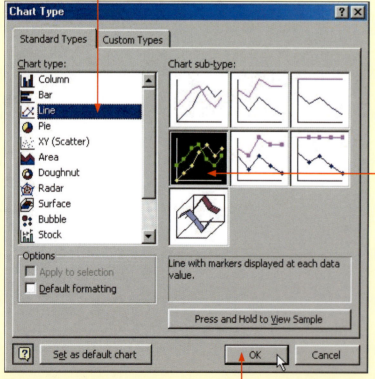

6 Select a **Chart sub-type**.

7 Click **OK**.

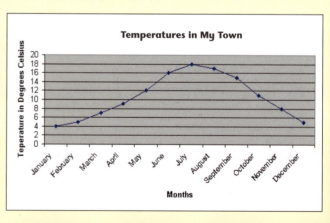

*Excel*Works

Change the Population Chart

SKILL: Changing the Chart Type

APPLICATION

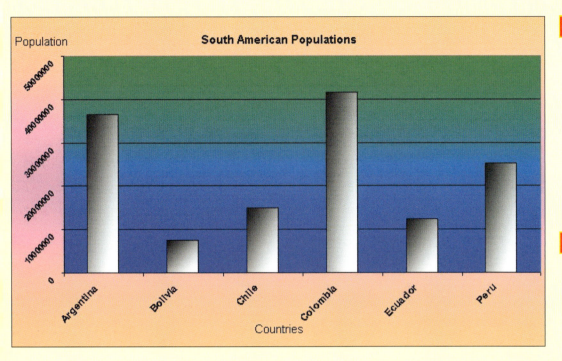

1 **Open** the workbook in which you saved the 'South American Populations' **Chart**. (See 29b)

2 Change the **Column Chart** to a **Bar Chart**. (See 30a)

3 Change the **Text Angle** of the text and numbers to make the **Bar Chart** look better. (See 29a)

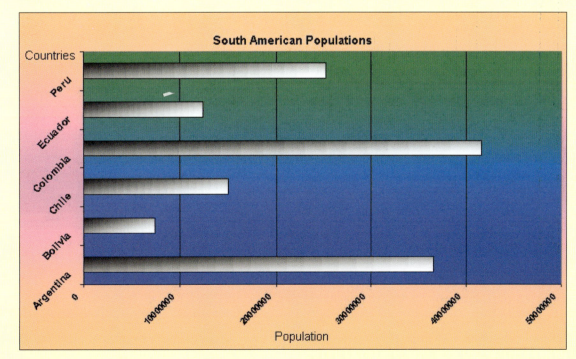

4 **Save** and **Print**.

Excel*Works*

31a

SKILL

1 **Open** an existing workbook containing a **Chart**.

2 Select the **Chart**.

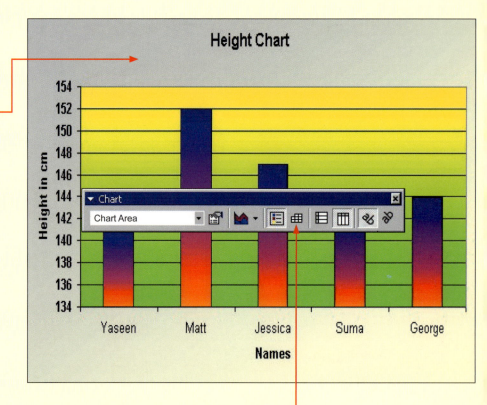

3 Click the **Data Table** icon on the **Chart** toolbar. The **Data Table** will now appear underneath your **Chart**.

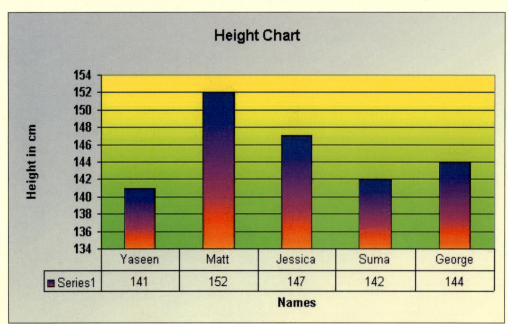

*Now I can **Print** my **Chart** and **Data Table** on one sheet.*

Excel*Works*

Add a Data Table to your Chart

31b

APPLICATION

1 **Open** the workbook in which you saved the 'South American Populations' **Chart**. (See 30b)

2 Add a **Data Table** to the **Chart**. (See 31a)

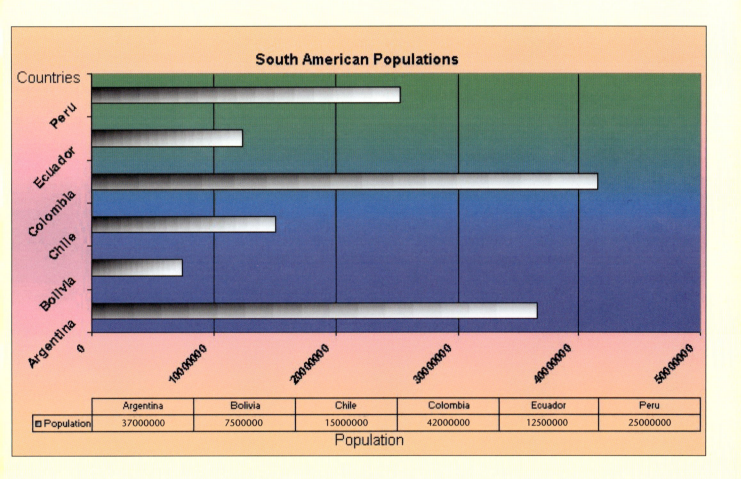

South American Populations

	Argentina	Bolivia	Chile	Colombia	Ecuador	Peru
▫ Population	37000000	7500000	15000000	42000000	12500000	25000000

Population

3 **Save** and **Print**.

Using the Addition Formula

32a

SKILL

> **Addition Formula: =First Cell address+Second Cell address**

1 Open a **New** workbook.

2 Enter the first number into a **Cell**.

3 Enter the second number into the **Cell** below.

A2	▼		=	35

	A	B	C
1	65		
2	35		
3			

65 + 35

4 Select the **Cell** below the numbers you want to add together.

	▼	✗ ✓	=	=A1+A2

	A	B	C	
1	65			
2	35			
3	=A1+A2			
4				

=A1+A2

5 Type the **Formula**:

 = | Cell address of First number | **+** | Cell address of Second number

6 Press **Enter**.

> **Remember**
> *Do not press the spacebar when typing your **Formula**.*
> *Always put the = sign first.*
> *The **Cell address** starts with the letter and the number follows, e.g. **A1**.*

A3	▼		=	=A1+A2

	A	B	C	D
1	65			
2	35			
3	100			
4				
5				

65 + 35 = 100

ExcelWorks

SKILL: Using the Addition Formula

APPLICATION

1 Open a **New** workbook.

2 Enter the following problems as additions in your workbook.

> **Remember**
> **Always** *use an = sign and do not leave spaces in the* **Formula**.

a. You buy a bag of crisps for 30p and chocolate bar for 35p.
How much have you spent?

b. You buy a CD for £13.99 and a DVD for £21.99.
How much have you spent?

c. For your birthday you receive £23 from your grandparents and £10 from your aunt.
How much do you get in total?

d. You buy a pair of jeans for £15.99 and a T-shirt for £9.99.
How much have you spent?

e. You buy a box of chocolates for £4.99 and a birthday card for £1.15.
What is the total?

3 Enter a **Formula** to calculate the answers. (See 32a)

4 **Save** and **Print**.

Using the Sum Formula

33a

SKILL

Formula: **=SUM(First Cell address:Last Cell address)**

1 Open a **New** workbook.

A3		=	10	
	A	**B**	**C**	**D**
1	10			
2	10			
3	10			
4				
5				

2 List the numbers you want to add in one **Column**.

3 Select the **Cell** below the numbers you want to add together.

10 + 10 + 10

SUM		X ✓ =	=SUM(A1:A3)	
	A	**B**	**C**	**D**
1	10			
2	10			
3	10			
4	=SUM(A1:A3)			

=SUM(A1:A3)

4 Type the **Formula**:

 =   **SUM**   **(**   **Cell address of First number**   **:**   **Cell address of Last number**   **)**

5 Press **Enter**.

Remember
Do not press the spacebar when typing your **Formula**. *Always put the = sign first. The* **Cell address** *starts with the letter and the number follows, e.g.* **A1**.

A4		=	=SUM(A1:A3)	
	A	**B**	**C**	**D**
1	10			
2	10			
3	10			
4	30			
5				

10 + 10 + 10 = 30

Excel*Works*

Pocket Money Budget

SKILL: Using the Sum Formula

1   Open a **New** workbook.

2   Enter the following problems as additions.

> ### Remember
> **Always** *use a = sign and do not leave spaces in the* **Formula**.

a.   You buy a CD for £12.99, a DVD for £18.99 and a video for £11.99.
How much do they cost in total?

b.   You buy a magazine for £2.99, a newspaper for 49p and a comic for £1.59
How much do they cost in total?

c.   You buy a packet of mints for 20p, a chocolate bar for 43p and a bag of crisps for 23p.
How much do they cost in total?

d.   You buy a T-shirt for £7.99, a pair of socks for £1.79 and a skirt for £17.
How much do they cost in total?

e.   You buy a pen for £1.50, an eraser for 87p and a pencil for 90p.
How much do they cost in total?

3   Enter a **Formula** to calculate the answer. (See 33a)

4   **Save** and **Print**.

Using AutoSum

1 Open a **New** workbook.

2 List the numbers you want to add in one **Column**.

	A	B	C
	A4	▼	= 43
1	10		
2	15		
3	20		
4	43		
5			

3 Select the **Cell** below the numbers you want to add together.

4 Click the **AutoSum** icon.

AutoSum

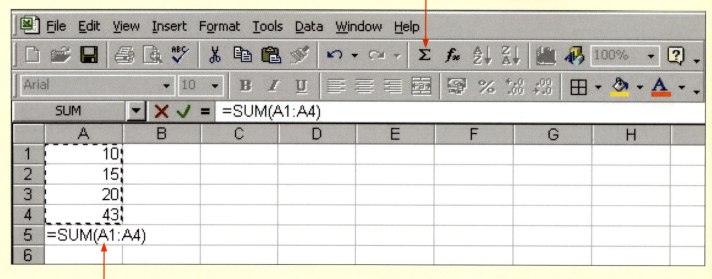

The **Formula** will now appear.

5 Press **Enter**.
The total will now appear.

	A	B	C	D
	A5	▼	= =SUM(A1:A4)	
1	10			
2	15			
3	20			
4	43			
5	88			
6				

$10 + 15 + 20 + 43 = 88$

1 Open a **New** workbook.

2 Enter the following problems.

a. It takes you five minutes to walk to the shop, you take ten minutes in the shop and five minutes to walk back.
What is the total time you spent?

b. You walk one kilometre to your friend's house, two kilometres into town and then three kilometres home.
How far have you walked?

c. You go on holiday and travel for 1 hour on the train, 3 hours on the plane and ½ hour on the bus to reach your hotel.
How long was your journey in minutes?

d. While on holiday, you spend $15 on a swimming costume, $10 at the water park, $25 at the amusement park and $45 on presents.
How much do you spend in total?

e. On your journey home, you spend $\frac{1}{2}$ hour on the bus, $3\frac{1}{2}$ hours on the plane, 1 hour at the railway station and $1\frac{1}{4}$ hours on the train.
How long does it take to get home in minutes?

3 Calculate the answers using **AutoSum**. (See 34a)

AutoSum

4 **Save** and **Print**.

Using the Subtraction Formula

Subtraction Formula: **=First Cell address–Second Cell address**

A2	▼		=	35
	A	**B**		**C**
1	65			
2	35			
3				

1 Open a **New** workbook.

2 Enter the first number into a **Cell**.

3 Enter the number you want to subtract from the first in the **Cell** below.

65 – 35

SUM	▼	✗ ✓ =	=A1-A2
	A	**B**	**C**
1	65		
2	35		
3	=A1-A2		
4			
5			

4 Select the **Cell** below the numbers you want to subtract.

=A1–A2

5 Type the **Formula**: **=** | Cell address of First number | **—** | Cell address of Second number |

6 Press **Enter**.

A3	▼		=	=A1-A2
	A	**B**		**C**
1	65			
2	35			
3	30			
4				
5				

65 – 35 = 30

Remember
*Do not leave spaces when typing your **Formula**. Always put the = sign first. The **Cell address** starts with the letter and the number follows, e.g. **A1**.*

35b

APPLICATION

1 Open a **New** workbook.

2 Enter the following problems as subtractions in your workbook.

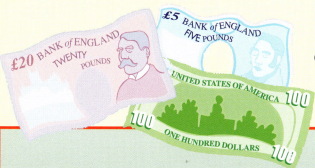

> **Remember**
> To **Format** the **Cells** to display
> **Currency** and two **Decimal places**.
> (See 12a)

Your local electrical store has a sale. Calculate the prices of the following items.

a. Colour *Gameboy* at £54.50 has a discount of £3.95.

b. 28cm TV at £190 has a discount of £29.

c. Video recorder at £114 has a discount of £15.25.

d. Desk lamp at £14.50 has a discount of £1.70.

e. CD player at £89.99 has a discount of £7.69.

f. Camera at €237.50 has a discount of €16.10.

g. *Playstation* at €324.95 has a discount of €11.50.

h. Personal Stereo at $50 has a discount of $10.60.

i. Computer system at $1919 has a discount of $108.40.

j. Mobile phone at £99.99 has a discount of £4.86.

3 Enter a **Formula** to calculate the answers. (See 35a)

4 **Save** and **Print**.

36a

SKILL

Using the Multiplication Formula

Multiplication Formula: **=First Cell address*Second Cell address**

The symbol for multiplication is *****.

1 Open a **New** workbook.

2 Enter the first number into a **Cell**.

3 Enter the number you want to multiply it by in the **Cell** below.

4 Select the **Cell** below.

A2	▼	=	35
	A	B	C
1	65		
2	35		
3			

65 x 35

SUM	▼	✗ ✓ =	=A1*A2
	A	B	C
1	65		
2	35		
3	=A1*A2		
4			
5			

=A1*A2

5 Type the **Formula**: **=** | Cell address of First number | ***** | Cell address of the Second number |

6 Press **Enter**.

A3	▼	=	=A1*A2
	A	B	C
1	65		
2	35		
3	2275		
4			
5			

65 x 35 = 2275

ExcelWorks

1   Open a **New** workbook.

2   Enter the following problems as multiplications in your workbook.

> **Remember**
> *Use* ✳ *as the multiplication symbol in* Excel.

You are buying stationery for your school. Calculate how much the items will cost.

a. 100 pencils at 5p each.

b. 50 pads of A4 lined paper at 75p each.

c. 100 pens at 17p each.

d. 167 packets of crayons at 89p each.

e. 55 rulers at 67p each.

f. 550 compasses at 40p each.

g. 99 packets of chalk at 55p each.

h. 220 erasers at 3p each.

i. 88 fountain pens at 89p each.

j. 5 ink cartridges at £23.99 each.

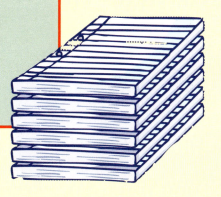

3   Enter a **Formula** to calculate the answers. (See 36a)

4   **Save** and **Print**.

Using the Division Formula

37a

SKILL

Division Formula: **=First Cell address/Second Cell address**

The symbol for division is **/**.

B2	▼	=	100
	A	B	C
1			
2	10	100	
3			
4			

100 ÷ 10

1 Open a **New** workbook.

2 Enter the first number into a **Cell**.

3 Enter the number you want to divide by in the **Cell** to the left.

4 Select the **Cell** below one of the numbers.

	▼	✗ ✓ =	=B2/A2
	A	B	C
1			
2	10	100	
3		=B2/A2	
4			

=B2/ A2

5 Type the **Formula**:   **/**

6 Press **Enter**.

*You can type the **Formula** in a **Cell** above, below or to the side of the numbers. The important thing is to get the **Cell addresses** correct.*

B3	▼	=	=B2/A2
	A	B	C
1			
2	10	100	
3		10	
4			

100 ÷ 10 = 10

Excel*Works*

Electrical Discounts

37b

APPLICATION

SKILL: Using the Division Formula

1 Open a **New** workbook.

2 Calculate the price of each item after the discounts have been made. (See 37a)

> **Remember**
> Use the **/** key for the division symbol in *Excel*.

Item	Cost	$\frac{1}{2}$ Price	$\frac{1}{3}$ Off
TV	£200.00		
Video	£150.00		
Computer	£800.00		
CD Player	£90.00		
Camera	£399.00		
DVD	£19.00		
MP3 Player	£259.00		
Fridge	£299.00		
Freezer	£319.00		
Dishwasher	£211.00		

3 **Save** and **Print**.

> **Remember**
> To **Format** the **Cells** to display **Currency** and two **Decimal Places**. (See 12a)

Using the Average Formula

38a

SKILL

Formula: **=Average(First Cell address:Last Cell address)**

*The **:** tells Excel to include the **Cells** between the first and the last **Cell** addresses in the calculation.*

A4	▼		=	90
	A	**B**	**C**	
1	60			
2	70			
3	80			
4	90			
5				

60, 70, 80, 90

1 Open a **New** workbook.

2 List the numbers you want to calculate the **Average** of in one **Column**.

3 Select the **Cell** below the list.

AVERAGE	▼	✗ ✓	=	=AVERAGE(A1:A4)	
	A	**B**	**C**	**D**	
1	60				
2	70				
3	80				
4	90				
5	=AVERAGE(A1:A4)				

=AVERAGE(A1:A4)

4 Enter the **Formula**:

 = | **Average** | **(** | **Cell address of First number** | **:** | **Cell address of Last number** | **)**

A5	▼		=	=AVERAGE(A1:A4)	
	A	**B**	**C**	**D**	
1	60				
2	70				
3	80				
4	90				
5	75				

5 Press **Enter**. Your answer will appear.

*The **Average** of 60, 70, 80 & 90 = 75*

Excel/Works

1 Open a **New** workbook.

2 Enter the following results for height and weight in your workbook.

Name	Height in cm	Weight in kg
Jane	148	42
Harry	146	39
Rajiv	140	32
Greta	155	50
Leroy	154	52
Augusta	137	31

3 Calculate the **Average** height of the group. (See 38a)

4 Calculate the **Average** weight of the group.

5 Enter the following results for hand spans and shoe sizes in your workbook.

6 Calculate the **Average** hand span of the group.

Name	Hand span in cm	Shoe Size
Jane	10	3
Harry	15	5
Rajiv	12	4
Greta	17	6
Leroy	19	7
Augusta	14	2

7 Calculate the **Average** shoe size of the group.

8 **Save** and **Print**.

Using the Minimum and Maximum Formulae

SKILL 39a

Minimum

Formula: =MIN(First Cell address:Last Cell address)

A4	▼		=	5092

	A	B	C
1	5029		
2	5192		
3	5290		
4	5092		
5			

1. Open a **New** workbook.

2. List these numbers in one **Column**.

3. Select the **Cell** below.

5029, 5192, 5290, 5092

4. Enter the **Formula**:

 = | **MIN** | **(** | **Cell address of First number** | **:** | **Cell address of Last number** | **)**

MIN	▼	✗ ✓	=	=MIN(A1:A4)

	A	B	C	D
1	5029			
2	5192			
3	5290			
4	5092			
5	=MIN(A1:A4)			

=MIN(A1:A4)

A5	▼		=	=MIN(A1:A4)

	A	B	C	D
1	5029			
2	5192			
3	5290			
4	5092			
5	5029			

*The **Minimum** value in the **Range** is 5029.*

5. Press **Enter**. The **Minimum** value will appear.

Maximum

Formula: =MAX(First Cell address:Last Cell address)

A5	▼		=	=MAX(A1:A4)

	A	B	C	D
1	5029			
2	5192			
3	5290			
4	5092			
5	5290			

6. When finding a **Maximum** value, replace **MIN** with **MAX** in the **Formula**.

7. Press **Enter**. The **Maximum** value will appear.

*The **Maximum** value in the **Range** is 5290.*

Excel Works

Calculate Minimum and Maximum Height and Weight

SKILL: Using the Minimum and Maximum Formulae

39b

APPLICATION

1 Open a **New** workbook.

2 Enter the following table in your workbook.

Name	Height in cm	Weight in kg
Kate	143	35
Philip	131	28
Rafiq	161	55
Golda	130	29
Winston	147	40
Michelle	154	49

3 Calculate who is the smallest, using the **Minimum Formula**. (See 39a)

4 Calculate who is the lightest, using the **Minimum Formula**.

5 Calculate who is the tallest, using the **Maximum Formula**.

6 Calculate who is the heaviest, using the **Maximum Formula**.

7 Enter the following table in your workbook.

8 Calculate who has the smallest hand span using the **Minimum Formula**.

9 Calculate who has the largest hand span using the **Maximum Formula**.

10 **Save** and **Print**.

Name	Hand span in cm
Kate	17
Philip	13
Rafiq	19
Golda	14
Winston	17
Michelle	18

Using Percentages

You can use the **Percent Style Format** and the **Multiplication Formula** to help you calculate the **Percentage** of any number.

If you want to calculate 15% of 45:

1 Open a **New** workbook.

2 Enter 45 in a **Cell**.

3 Select the **Cell** to the right.

4 Click **Format**.

5 Click **Cells**.

6 Click the **Number** tab.

7 Click **Percentage**.

8 Click **OK**.

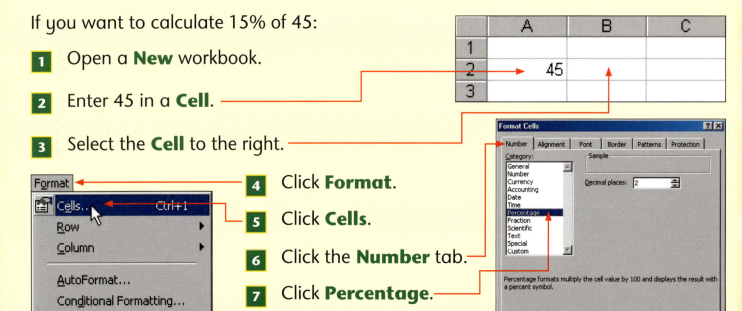

9 Enter 15 in the **Cell**.

10 Select the **Cell** to the right.

11 Enter the **Multiplication Formula**. (See 36a)

| = | Cell address of First number | * | Cell address of the Second number |

12 Press **Enter**. Your answer will appear.

*What if I want to find a **Percentage** of an amount of money?*

- Before you enter the number, select the **Cell** and click the **Currency** icon. (See 12a)

- Follow instructions **2** to **12**.
  Your answer will appear with a Currency symbol.

Currency

Calculate Class Attendance

SKILL: Using Percentages

40b

APPLICATION

1 Open a **New** workbook.

2 Copy the class attendance table into your workbook.

> *Remember*
> Always **Format** the **Cells** to show **Percentages** before you enter the values.

3 Format the **Cells** in the **% Attendance Column** to show **Percentages**. (See 40a)

	A	B	C	D	E
1					
2					
3			Total Pupils in Class	% Attendance	Pupils Present
4		Class 1	30	90%	
5		Class 2	33	100%	
6		Class 3	36	75%	
7		Class 4	30	70%	
8		Class 5	35	60%	
9		Class 6	25	92%	
10					

4 Calculate the number of pupils present in each class, using the **Multiplication Formula**. (See 40a)

5 **Save** and **Print**.

> *You can **Format Cells** to show **Percentages** using the **Percent Style** icon.*

● Before you enter your values, select the **Cell** and click the **Percent Style** icon.

Percent Style

ExcelWorks

41a

SKILL

Calculating Percentages

Formula: **=Cell address of X/Cell address of Y**

*This **Formula** calculates what **Percentage** one number (X) is of another number (Y) when you enter it in a **Cell** that is formatted to show **Percentages**.*

If you want to find out what **Percentage** 10 (X) is of 50 (Y):

1 Open a **New** workbook.

2 Type 50 (**Y** value) into a **Cell**.

3 Type 10 (**X** value) into the **Cell** to the right.

	A	B
1		
2	50	10

50, 10

4 Select the **Cell** below and click the **Percent Style** icon to **Format** the **Cell**.

▼ ✗ ✓ = =B2/A2

	A	B	C
1			
2	50	10	
3		=B2/A2	

=B2/A2

5 Enter the **Formula**: **=** Cell address of X **/** Cell address of Y

6 Press **Enter**. Your answer will appear.

B3 ▼ = =B2/A2

	A	B	C
1			
2	50	10	
3		20%	

10 is 20% of 50

Excel*Works*

Reduced Electrical Goods

SKILL: Calculating Percentages

APPLICATION

1 Open a **New** workbook.

2 Enter the following table in your workbook.

	A	B	C	D	E	F
1						
2		Item	Price	Sale Price	Discount	% Reduction
3		TV	£200	£150	£50	25%
4		Hi-fi	£499	£390		
5		Video	£199	£150		
6		Computer	£900	£850		
7		Fridge	£250	£118		
8		Freezer	£310	£234		
9		Dishwasher	£290	£132		
10		Microwave	£89	£65		
11						

3 Use the subtraction **Formula** to calculate the discount for each item in pounds. (See 35a)

4 Now calculate the discount for each item as a **Percentage**.
The easiest way to do this is to calculate what **Percentage** the discount is of the original price. (See 41a)

Example:
The first set of calculations is done for you.
To find what **Percentage** £50 is of £200,
type the following **Formula** in **F3**:
E2/C2
The answer is 25%.

5 **Save** and **Print**.

Using the Paste Function

Many **Formulae** have been created for you in *Excel*. They are called **Functions**.

1 Open a **New** workbook.

2 Type your numbers.

3 Select the **Cell** where you want to enter the **Formula**.

4 Click **Insert**.

5 Click **Function**.

6 Click **Statistical**.

*I can also use the **Paste Function** icon on the toolbar.*

Paste Function

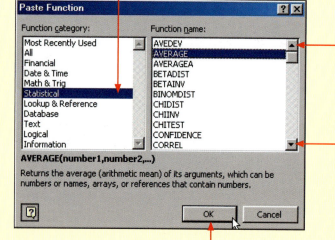

7 Click the arrows to look through the **Function names**.

8 Click the **Function** you want. The **Average** function is shown here.

9 Click **OK**.

10 Check to see that your **Range** is correct. If it is incorrect, drag your mouse over the **Range** of values you wish to find the **Average** of.

11 Click **OK**.

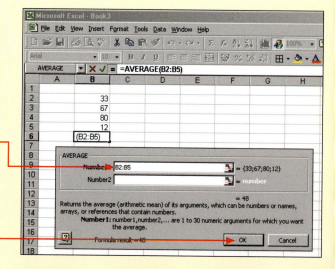

*Excel*Works

Find the Average Temperature

SKILL: Using the Paste Function

42b
APPLICATION

1 Open a **New** workbook.

2 Enter the following information in your workbook.

	A	B	C	D	E	F	
1							
2		**Temperature in the playground at 9:00am during January (in °C)**					
3							
4			**Week 1**	**Week 2**	**Week 3**	**Week 4**	
5		Monday	0	1	2	4	
6		Tuesday	1	3	0	1	
7		Wednesday	0	4	1	2	
8		Thursday	2	2	1	0	
9		Friday	3	2	0	1	
10							

3 Use the **Paste Function** icon to calculate the **Average** temperature for week 1. (See 42a)

Paste Function

4 Find the **Average** temperature for week 2, week 3 and week 4.

5 Find the **Average** temperature for all 20 days.
To do this, drag the mouse across the **Range** (**Cells C5** to **F9**) when you reach the stage where you check the **Range**.

6 **Save** and **Print**.

43a SKILL

Using the Paste Function to Find the Median

The **Median** is the middle value in a **Range** of values in numerical order.

1 Open a **New** workbook.

2 Enter your numbers in the same **Column**.

3 Select the **Cell** where you want your answer to appear.

4 Click **Insert**.

5 Click **Function**.

6 Click **Statistical**.

7 Click **Median**.

8 Click **OK**.

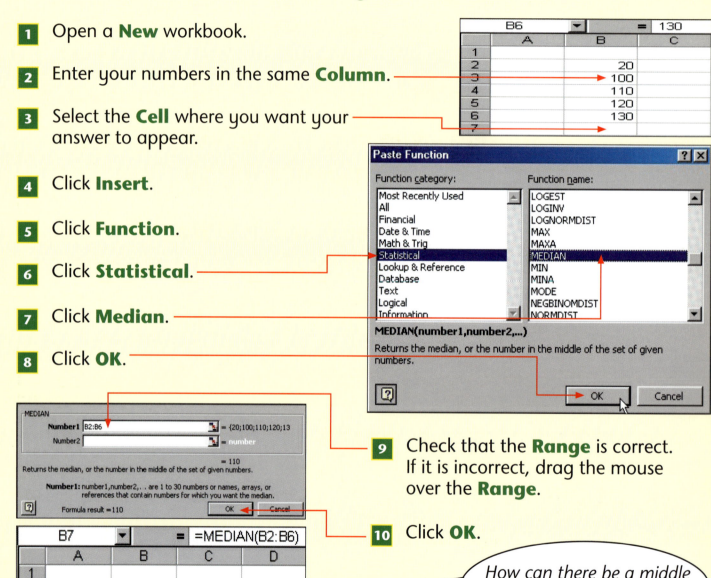

9 Check that the **Range** is correct. If it is incorrect, drag the mouse over the **Range**.

10 Click **OK**.

> *How can there be a middle value if you have an even number of values?*

The **Median** value of 20, 100, 110, 120 and 130 is 110.

● When there is an even number of values in a **Range**, *Excel* will calculate the **Average** of the middle pair as the **Median** value, for example the **Median** value of 2, 7, 9, 10 is 8.

Find the Median Temperature

SKILL: Using the Paste Function to Find the Median

APPLICATION

1 Open a **New** workbook.

2 Enter the following table in your workbook.

	A	B	C	D	E	F
1						
2		Temperature in the playground at noon during June (in °C)				
3						
4			Week 1	Week 2	Week 3	Week 4
5		Monday	20	17	16	18
6		Tuesday	18	18	17	21
7		Wednesday	19	19	18	24
8		Thursday	15	21	19	23
9		Friday	18	20	20	22

3 Use the **Paste Function** icon to calculate the **Median** temperature for week 1. (See 43a)

Paste Function

4 Find the **Median** temperature for week 2, week 3 and week, 4.

5 Find the **Median** temperature for all 20 days.
To do this, drag the mouse across the **Range** (**Cells C5** to **F9**) when you reach the stage where you check the **Range**.

6 **Save** and **Print**.

Excel*Works*

44a

SKILL

Using the Paste Function to Find the Mode

The **Mode** is the value that occurs most often in a **Range** of values.

1 Open a **New** workbook.

2 Enter your numbers in one **Column**.

3 Select the **Cell** where you want your answer to appear.

4 Click **Insert**.

5 Click **Function**.

6 Click **Statistical**.

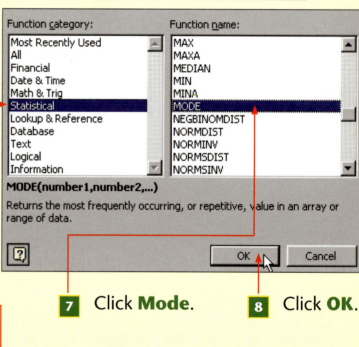

7 Click **Mode**.

8 Click **OK**.

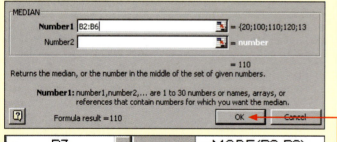

9 Check that the **Range** is correct. If it is incorrect, drag the mouse over the **Range**.

10 Click **OK**.

The **Mode** *value of 60, 60, 70, 90, 60 is 60.*

Excel**Works**

Find the Mode Temperature

SKILL: Using the Paste Function to Find the Mode

44b

APPLICATION

1 Open a **New** workbook.

2 Enter the following table in your workbook.

	A	B	C	D	E	F
1						
2		Temperature in the playground at noon during September (in °C)				
3						
4			Week 1	Week 2	Week 3	Week 4
5		Monday	19	22	14	16
6		Tuesday	15	21	16	15
7		Wednesday	18	19	17	14
8		Thursday	15	21	16	11
9		Friday	25	15	18	11

3 Use the **Paste Function** icon to calculate the **Mode** temperature for week 1. (See 44a)

Paste Function

4 Find the **Mode** temperatures for week 2, week 3 and week 4.

5 Find the **Mode** temperature for September.
To do this, drag the mouse across the 20 temperatures when you reach the stage where you check the **Range**.

6 **Save** and **Print**.

Using Cut and Paste

1 **Open** an existing workbook.

2 Select the **Cell** you want to **Cut**.

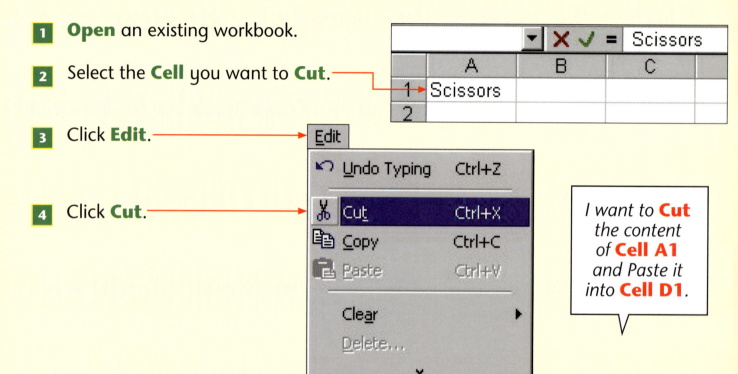

3 Click **Edit**.

4 Click **Cut**.

> I want to **Cut** the content of **Cell A1** and Paste it into **Cell D1**.

5 Click where you want your **Cell** to be **Pasted**.

6 Click **Edit**.

7 Click **Paste**.

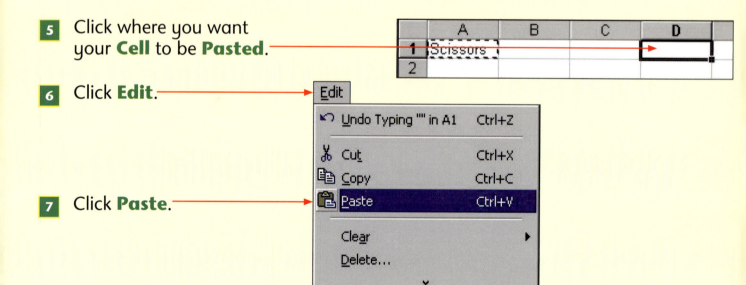

Excel/Works

Sort Data in Columns

SKILL: Using Cut and Paste

45b

APPLICATION

1 Open a **New** workbook.

2 Type a list of 10 members of your class in **Column A**.

3 **Cut** and **Paste** the boys in your class into **Column B**. (See 45a)

4 **Cut** and **Paste** the girls in your class into **Column C**.

5 Try this again using the **Cut** and **Paste** icons on the toolbar.

6 **Fill** the **Boys** and **Girls Columns** with a **Colour** of your choice.

	A	B	C
1	Joanne	Boys	Girls
2	Kevin		
3	Lisa		
4	Phillip		
5	Mohsin		
6	Fatima		
7	Christopher		
8	Kelly		
9	Bethany		
10	David		
11			
12			

Cut

Paste

	A	B	C
1		Boys	Girls
2		Kevin	Joanne
3		Phillip	Lisa
4		Mohsin	Fatima
5		Christopher	Kelly
6		David	Bethany

7 **Save** and **Print**.

46a

SKILL

Using Copy and Paste

1 **Open** an existing workbook in which you saved calculations.

2 Select the **Cell** containing the **Formula** that you want to **Copy**. The **Formula** is displayed in the **Formula Bar**.

3 Click **Edit**.

4 Click **Copy**.

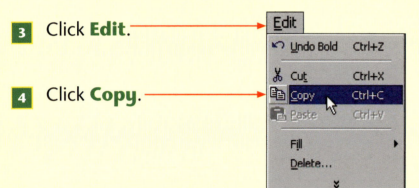

5 Select the **Cell** where you want the **Formula** to be **Pasted**.

6 Click **Edit**.

7 Click **Paste**.

*When you **Paste** the **Formula** in the **Cell**, the **Cell addresses** adjust to make the **Formula** apply to the new location.*

● The **Formula** will now be **Pasted** into the current **Cell**, to give the correct answer.

*Excel*Works

Copy a Formula to Calculate Costs

SKILL: Using Copy and Paste

APPLICATION

1 Open a **New** workbook.

2 Enter the following data in your workbook.

> *Make sure you* **Format** *the Cells in* **Column B** *and* **Column D** *to show the* **Currency**.

	A	B	C	D
1	*Fruit*	*Price of each (in £)*	*Quantity bought*	*Cost = Price*Quantity*
2	Apples	£0.20	6	
3	Pears	£0.17	9	
4	Oranges	£0.40	5	
5	Plums	£0.10	12	
6			*Total Cost of Fruit*	

3 Enter a **Formula** in **Cell D2** to calculate the cost of the apples. (See 37a)

4 **Copy** the **Formula** that you have entered. (See 46a)

5 Highlight **Cells D3 – D5**.

6 **Paste** the **Formula** in the highlighted **Cells**.

7 Calculate the total cost of the fruit using **AutoSum** in **Cell D6**. (See 34a)

8 **Save** and **Print**.

Scatter Charts are used to compare two sets of values to see if they are related.

You are going to create a graph showing how the heights and weights of some children are related.

	A	B	C
1	Height cm	Weight kg	
2	152	45	
3	148	43	
4	155	45	
5	159	50	
6	144	43	
7	157	48	
8	146	44	
9			

1 Open a **New** workbook and add the table opposite.

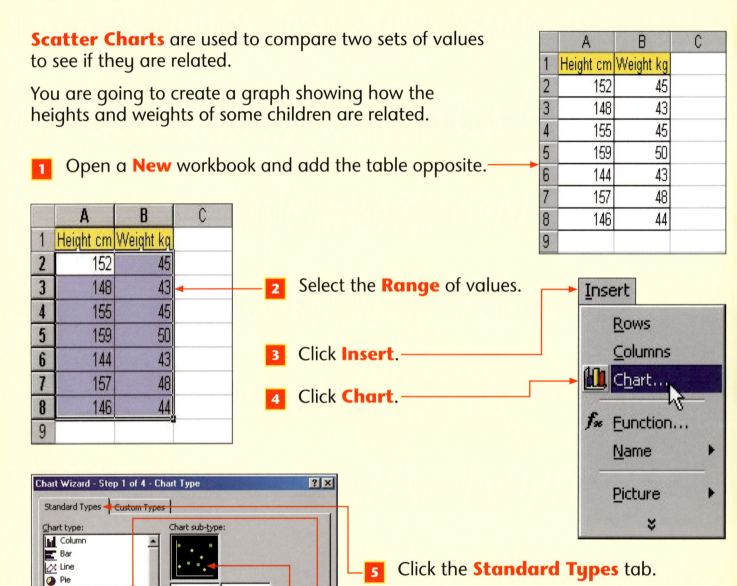

2 Select the **Range** of values.

3 Click **Insert**.

4 Click **Chart**.

5 Click the **Standard Types** tab.

6 Click **XY (Scatter)**.

7 Select a **Chart sub-type**.

8 Click and hold to **View Chart**.

9 Click **Next**.

(continued on page 103)

10 View the **Scatter Chart**.

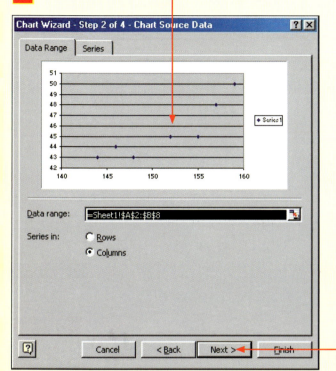

Each point shows the height and weight of one person. You can see that taller people usually weigh more.

11 Click **Next**.

12 Click the **Titles** tab.

13 Enter the **Chart title**.

14 Click and enter a title for the **X-axis**.

15 Click and enter a title for the **Y-axis**.

16 Click the **Legend** tab.

17 Click to remove the **Legend**.

*You can use **Titles**, **Axes**, **Gridlines**, and **Legend** to improve the appearance of the **Chart**.*

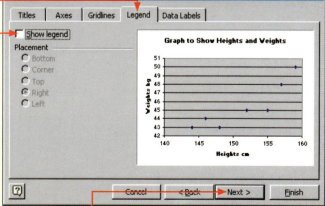

18 Click **Next**.

(continued on page 104)

*Excel*Works

19 Choose a **Chart Location**.

*Your **Chart** can appear on a **New Sheet**, or as an object on the **Sheet** you are working on.*

20 Click **Finish**.

The **Scatter Chart** will now be completed.

21 **Save** and **Print**.

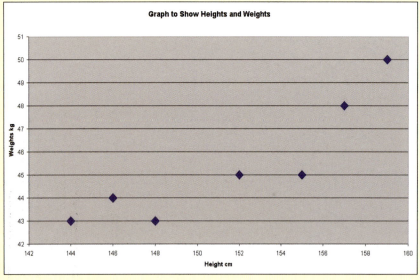

22 Try changing the **Colour of the Line**, **Chart Area** and **Plot Area**.

*You can make the **Data Point Markers** bigger by double-clicking on them and increasing the **Marker Size**.*

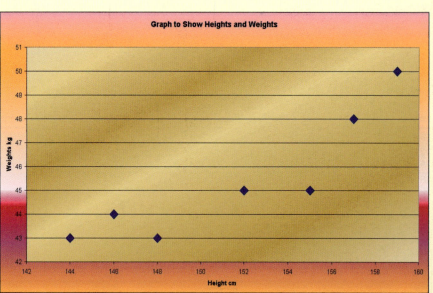

ExcelWorks

48

SKILL & APPLICATION

1 Open the workbook in which you saved your 'Class Pets' **Chart**. (See 24)

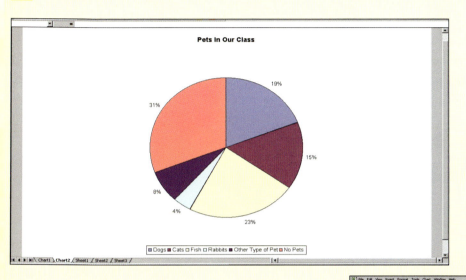

2 Change your **Pie Chart** to a **Column Chart**. (See 30a)

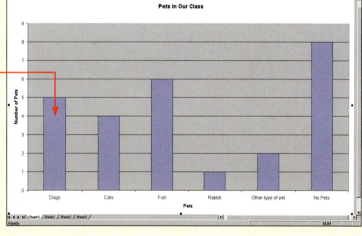

3 Double-click on the first one of the **Data Points** (Dogs).

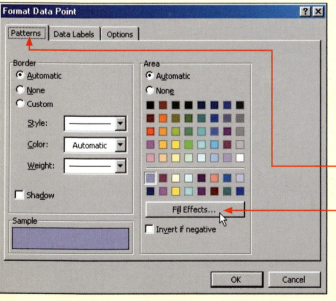

4 Click the **Patterns** tab.

5 Click **Fill Effects**.

(continued on page 106)

ExcelWorks

6   Click **Picture**.

7   Click **Select Picture**.

8   Click on the arrow.
A list of locations will appear.

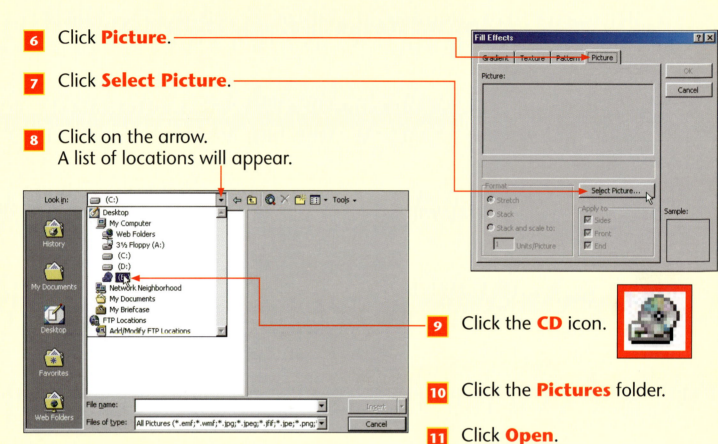

9   Click the **CD** icon.

10   Click the **Pictures** folder.

11   Click **Open**.

12   Click the **Picture** that you want.

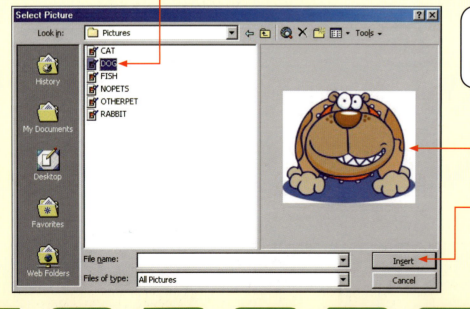

*Use the pet images
on the **ExcelWorks CD**
to complete the **Pictogram**.*

13   **Preview** the **Picture**.

14   Click **Insert**.

(continued on page 107)

48

SKILL & APPLICATION

15 Click **Stack and scale to**. (Check it is set to **1**)

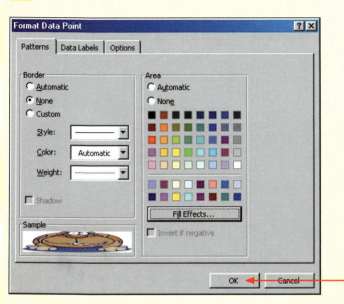

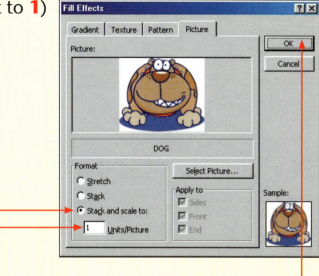

17 Click **OK**.

16 Click **OK**.

18 Add a **Picture** to each of your **Columns**.

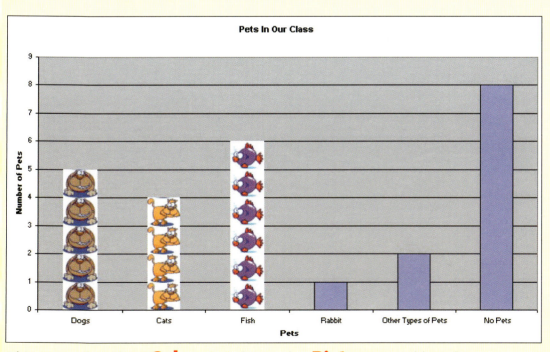

*This screen has three **Columns** changed to **Pictures** and has three* **Columns** *left to change.*

19 **Save** and **Print**.

*Excel*Works

Using AutoFormat

1 **Open** a workbook in which you have saved a data table.

	A	B	C	D	E	F	G	H
1								
2		**Total Monthly Rainfall (in mm)**						
3								
4		Weather Station	Jan	Feb	Mar	Apr	Total	
5		Armagh	36	43	55	63	197	
6		Bradford	53	93	48	89	283	
7		Lerwick	78	140	95	65	378	
8		Southampton	98	84	131	71	384	
9		Total	265	360	329	288	1242	
10								

2 Select the table.

3 Click **Format**.

Format

📋	C̲ells...	Ctrl+1
	R̲ow	▶
	C̲olumn	▶
	S̲heet	▶
	A̲utoFormat...	
	St̲yle...	
	⌄	

4 Click **AutoFormat**.

5 Choose a style.

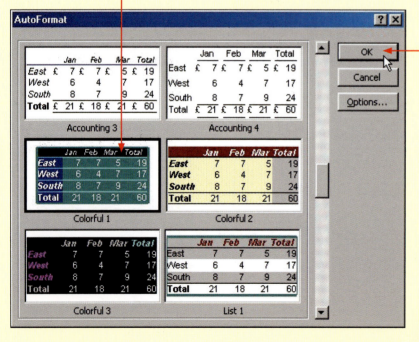

6 Click **OK**.

The table will now be formatted.

	A	B	C	D	E	F	G	H
1								
2		**Total Monthly Rainfall (in mm)**						
3								
4		**Weather Station**	Jan	Feb	Mar	Apr	Total	
5		Armagh	36	43	55	63	197	
6		Bradford	53	93	48	89	283	
7		Lerwick	78	140	95	65	378	
8		Southampton	98	84	131	71	384	
9		Total	265	360	329	288	1242	
10								

Favourite Hobbies

SKILL: Using AutoFormat

APPLICATION

1 Open a **New** workbook.

2 Make a table that shows a list of five pupils and their favourite hobbies.

	A	B	C
1			
2		Name	Hobby
3		Stuart	Football
4		Sarah	Swimming
5		Reena	Collecting Stamps
6		Muhammad	Fishing
7		Sammy	Reading

3 Make another table that shows a list of five more pupils and their favourite hobbies.

4 Use **AutoFormat** to change the appearance of the tables. (See 49a)

	A	B	C	D	E	F
1						
2		*Name*	*Hobby*		*Name*	*Hobby*
3		Stuart	Football		Alex	Astronomy
4		Sarah	Swimming		Mary	Playing Piano
5		Reena	Collecting Stamps		Yusra	Skateboarding
6		Muhammad	Fishing		Zia	Reading
7		Sammy	Reading		Rebecca	Computer Games

5 **Save** and **Print**.

6 Try this again but make a table of teachers and their favourite hobbies.

1. **Open** an existing workbook.

2. Find the **Format Painter** icon on your screen.

Format Painter

*You can use **Format Painter** to **Copy** a **Cell's Format** to other **Cells**.*

3. Select the **Cells** whose **Format** you want to **Copy**.

4. Click the **Format Painter** icon.

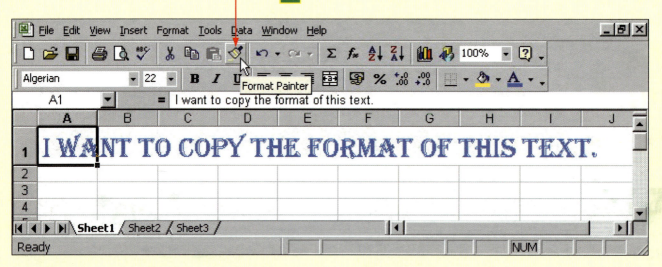

5. Select the **Cell** to which you want to apply the **Format**.

6. Enter your data.

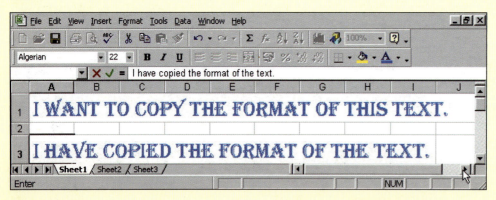

7. Click the **Format Painter** icon again to **Cancel**.

Excel*Works*

Shapes and Sizes

SKILL: Using Format Painter

50b

APPLICATION

1 Open the workbook in which you saved your minimum and maximum work. (See 39b)

2 Use **AutoFormat** to **Format** the first table. (See 49a)

3 Select the **Format** of the first table.

Name	Height in cm	Weight in kg
Kate	143	35
Philip	131	28
Rafiq	161	55
Golda	130	29
Winston	147	40
Michelle	154	49
Minimum	130	28
Maximum	161	55

4 Use **Format Painter** to change the other tables to the same style. (See 50a)

Name	Height in cm	Weight in kg
Kate	143	35
Philip	131	28
Rafiq	161	55
Golda	130	29
Winston	147	40
Michelle	154	49
Minimum	130	28
Maximum	161	55

Name	Hand span in cm
Kate	17
Philip	13
Rafiq	19
Golda	14
Winston	17
Michelle	18
Minimum	13
Maximum	19

5 **Save** and **Print**.

ExcelWorks

Photocopying

Please note that pages from this book may **NOT** be photocopied.

The CLA licence does **NOT** apply to this book.

© 2002 Folens Limited, on behalf of the authors.
United Kingdom: Folens Publishers, Apex Business Centre, Boscombe Road, Dunstable, LU5 4RL.
Email: folens@folens.com

Ireland: Folens Publishers, Greenhills Road, Tallaght, Dublin 24.
Email: info@folens.ie

Poland: JUKA, ul. Renesansowa 38, Warsaw 01-905.

Editor: Emma Thomas
Layout artists: Patricia Hollingsworth
Cover design: Patricia Harrison and Martin Cross
Illustrations: Jim Peacock

First published 2002 by Folens Limited.
Reprinted 2002.

Screenshots reprinted by permission from Microsoft Corporation.

Microsoft® and Excel are either registered trademarks or trademarks of Microsoft Corporation in the United States and other countries.

Microsoft Excel software is © 1985–1999 Microsoft Corporation. All rights reserved.

Page 108: Weather Station data taken from *The Met Office* website URL: http://www.metoffice.gov.uk © Crown copyright 2002.

Every effort has been made to trace the copyright holders of material used in this publication. If any copyright holder has been overlooked, we should be pleased to make any necessary arrangements.

British Library Cataloguing in Publication Data. A catalogue record for this publication is available from the British Library.

ISBN 1 84303 137 X